Animal Communication

with

All Species

Holly Davis

DEDICATION

A massive 'Thank you' to all the animals who have
made my life what it is today - to my friends and
family for their support. Also to all my various
teachers - be they two or four legged, who have
enabled me to learn from them and have shared
their time will me. Without all of you, this book
would not have been in print today.

To the animals....
I am sorry that so many people do not listen to
you....
That so many ignore your cries....
But I am trying to help you to be heard, each and
everyday.

*"We must educate our children to enable love and compassion
for all living things.
By doing this we can create a peaceful future for all."*

ACKNOWLEDGEMENTS

Sammi Pease – Mojo and Lola
Cover Photograph

Susan and Tim Duckworth
at Bitless and Barefoot

Andree Ralph – Free Spirit Ponies

Nicola Bebb

Andrea Platt Photography
www.andreaplattphotography.com

A huge 'Thank you' to you all !

*I asked a cat about what he thought about Animal
Communication - this was his reply....*

'It's not how, when, or why it works - it's the fact it does!'
'Guts' A Cat from Essex

.

CONTENTS

Introduction...................................4

1. What is Animal Communication?..................7
2. Clearing Negative Thought Patterns..........11
3. Meditation...................................18
4. How We Receive Information..................24
5. The Animal/Human Connection.................30
6. What Animals Know...........................36
7. How to Interpret...........................52
8. Conducting a Session.......................60
9. Body Scanning..............................76
10. Earth Energies............................85
11. Working with Other Therapists.............89
12. What are We Really Telling Them?..........103
13. Ethics and Legalities.....................108
14. The Animals' Prayer.......................115
15. Tracking Lost and Stolen Animals..........117
16. Choose Your Title Carefully...............126
17. Are Animals Psychic or Intuitive?.........134
18. Why Ask for Questions.....................140
19. Assessing Pain Levels.....................143
20. The Fine Line of Diagnosing...............146
21. The Selective Communicator................154
22. Autism, Learning Difficulties and Dementia157
23. The Psychological Safety Zone..............163
24. Save Them All Syndrome....................170
25. Looking Glass Syndrome....................180
26. Sympathy vs Empathy.......................186

About the Author.........................191

Freda.......................................194

INTRODUCTION

Animal Communication has been around for many thousands of years. In past times it was seen as normal for people to talk with their animal friends, but in our modern age of computers and conventional medicine, many of us have denied or ignored our natural abilities. For many people, animal communication is something that only the 'gifted few' can achieve. This of course is entirely untrue as we were all born with the ability to talk to and hear animals. For many children, talking to animals is a normal part of life but, as they grow up, they are seen as fanciful and imaginative to the point they start to believe that this is true and their abilities start to dwindle.

We can all learn to communicate with animals at any time in our lives. When we choose to communicate in such a way, we need to be relaxed so that our mind through our brainwave state is more open and receptive.

The mental state we are in when we communicate is very similar to self-hypnosis. This is brought about through meditation. As you progress, through practice, you will find that you can switch into this mind state very quickly and with ease. Almost like flicking a switch in brain that takes you from one part of your mind to another almost instantly.

Have you ever experienced driving in your car and missing a turning because your mind was focused on something else, only to have an animal run out in front of you and you snap back into the here and now?
If you have then what you experienced is very similar to the mind state needed to communicate with animals. It is very important to take a step back and look at why we wish to communicate with animals.

What set you on this path?

Have you encountered a sick animal that you wished you could have helped more?

Have you witnessed behaviour problems in animals and wished that you could understand them better?

Do you feel emotional for no obvious reason when in the presence of an animal?

When we communicate with animals it is very important that we work from the heart.

During communication, animals can feel our energy, compassion and intention so the more open and understanding we are, the more approachable we will make ourselves.

There are many things that animal communication can be useful for:

Finding the cause of behaviour problems

Finding sore and uncomfortable areas within the physical body

Emotional problems and the cause

Checking the fitting of equipment, such as saddles and collars

Helping to understand pet/owner relationships and how the animal feels.

Finding illnesses before they physically present themselves

Finding out how the animal feels about their environment, food and lifestyle.

WHAT IS ANIMAL COMMUNICATION?

Animal Communication is the ability to read the vibration frequencies that are held within the animals' electromagnetic energy field, often referred to as the 'Aura'.

Each thought, feeling and illness carries its own unique vibrational signature.

The ability to connect in this way and to hear animals talking, is often referred to as telepathy. In recent years there has been some confusion as many Communicators have chosen to call themselves cat/dog/horse whisperers. 'Whispering' refers to the art of reading the minute body signals that the animal gives off and their communication on a physical level. Animal communication is very different as the connection is purely mind to mind -

energy to energy.

There are several other different titles used by Animal Communicators including: Pet Psychic and Telepathic Pet Communicator - all of which essentially come down to the same thing.

When we are reading the vibrational frequencies, our subconscious takes that information in and stores it whilst translating it into words, pictures and feelings. This information is then transferred to our conscious self in a way that we can understand. It is down to the individual exactly how this information is received. Some 'feel' the information or physical ailments, some see only pictures and some only hear the information through words. Most of us will receive the information through a collection of these, to varying degrees. Many Animal Communicators never hear words being spoken but the feelings and pictures are very strong, so their information is just as clear as if they were hearing the animal speak using actual words.

Often when an animal has a problem, it can be viewing things from a negative perspective, or not be able to see the bigger picture. Through communication we can talk to and council an animal in exactly the same way as we would a person. Sometimes just this alone is enough to break a cycle of unwanted behavior, by opening them up to a new perspective and understanding. Some animals just benefit from knowing that someone (you) are willing to listen and is there for them.

Shamanic Animal Communication

Shamanic Animal Communication is slightly different as when working with an animal in this way, we work with the help of a compassionate animal spirit. The term Shaman (referring to the person who practices Shamanism) comes from Siberia, Tuva and Mongolia and is used to describe the person who practices the art of working with Animal Guides and venturing into the unseen realms. This often includes both guidance from the Animal Guides as well as them passing on information relating physical health, healing and how any problems may be addressed. Therefore, Shamans are typically seen as Medicine Men. Shamanism is used extensively by the indigenous people, as well as many folk cultures all over the world.

Transpersonal Interspecies Communication

This is the ability to communicate will all living things and their energy fields. By this I mean everything and anything living. Everything living has an electromagnetic energy field. This means that they have the ability to store information within their field that we can read. When we are communicating with this 'part' of the living being, what we are actually communicating with is a higher consciousness/part of their intelligence.

Transpersonal in simple terms could be interpreted as 'trans' - meaning in transit and 'personal' as in personal to that individual.

This leaves us with a very good description of this part of the consciousness, as this part is often in transit, not being connected directly to the physical. It is a form of energy, as indeed all consciousness is. It has the ability to move in and out of the physical body and to be sent to all corners of the universe in order to gather information.

The transpersonal self is often referred to as the 'higher-self' or 'over-soul'.

Transmigration

The migration or leaving of this part of the consciousness (in transit) that often involves the moving in, or attachment to another physical body.

Trans-Integration

The integration of this aspect of the consciousness attaching to the physical body. Also, to the energy systems of the individual and choosing to work with and through them.

CLEARING NEGATIVE THOUGHT PATTERNS

Many of us have self-doubt associated with our ability to communicate with animals. Sometimes this will have come through lack of confidence or low self-esteem. If we are having problems communicating then we first need to analyse the reasons behind it. As much as many people want to communicate with animals, some may also have an underlying fear of what they may hear. When communicating with our own animals we have a deeper emotional connection. When we are worried and concerned about them, we can sub-consciously block what it is we are hearing from them, as a way of safe-guarding ourselves and our own emotions. Whilst this can sometimes appear helpful, it is really only blocking what we really need to hear in order to help both ourselves, and our animals. By acknowledging our fear and seeing beyond it, we open ourselves up more widely to hearing what it is we truly need to hear. Many people experience the same kind of problems when trying to communicate with wild animals and those animals living with other people.

There can be many different reasons for why this is, but often the underlying reason is fear and discomfort. Many of us grow up being conditioned to believe in certain things. The problem being that when we choose to believe in one thing it can open up a whole chain of other beliefs being questioned.

Since communicating with animals may be the first link in this chain, we may block our abilities we have for communicating for fear of opening up a whole can of worms. Once we find ourselves communicating, we are open to hearing things that challenge those beliefs and make us question everything we had trusted and learned up until this time.

Examples

Your pet trying to tell you that they are ready to die

Your pet telling you they are very ill

Your pet telling you that they no longer want to live with you.

The Chatterbox

Many of you would have experienced what I refer to as the 'chatterbox'. This is the self-destructive part of us. The part of us that tells us 'we aren't good enough' and repeatedly tells us 'no you can't do that', or 'no you're wrong, you can't possibly be hearing correctly'. I'm sure many of you will be able to relate to this and will have experienced it at some point. The subconscious part of our minds is very easily fooled and is subservient to our conscious mind. That is to say that if we are told something often enough or repeatedly, we think negatively about ourselves. We will in time convince ourselves that it is indeed true as our subconscious will come to believe it.

The important thing to remember is that as the chatterbox is part of our make-up, we will never be able to rid ourselves of it, only lessen it. The best way that this can be achieved is to firstly recognise when it is our chatterbox speaking, rather than our authentic self. So everything your mind tells you something about yourself that is negative or upsetting in anyway, it should be dismissed as it is your chatterbox speaking. Every-time you hear this voice replace the negative with a positive.

Chatterbox

'I'm mad! Of course I can't hear animals speaking

only special people can'.

The True You

' I know I have the ability to hear animals speaking. The human and animal kingdoms are connected so that I can do this willingly and with ease'.

Once we start to fight back at our chatterbox it will usually accept this as a challenge. It may well be the case that it will choose to rear its head much more frequently. So long as we keep replacing the negative with a positive we can train our subconscious into a new way of thinking. In time our chatterbox will start to take much more of a back seat and we will hear it much less frequently.

The Belief System

As we can see, the human brain is an exceptionally complex tool. We carry certain beliefs through our life time that remain there, as they have never been challenged. In animal communication this can pose a problem for many different reasons. If we do not allow ourselves to communicate without judgment and not truly listen to what we are being told, we will never hear what is being said in its entirety. If we have already made a decision as to what is right or wrong for an animal, those beliefs can and will override what it is that we should be hearing. The reason for this again lies in our subconscious. By hearing something that doesn't agree with our own beliefs we are taken out of our comfort zone which for many people takes them into un-chartered waters and quite literally out of their depth. Choosing not to hear it and replacing it with a version of our own truth, is the obvious route it takes as a way yet again of trying to keep us mentally safe. When we choose to override our fear and let go of the egotistical part of us that tells us that we are always right, we leave ourselves open to hearing what the animal is truly saying.

The Ego in Perspective

When we first start to communicate it can be a very life changing experience. For some of us it will be a very gradual process. For others it can be very quick and full blown in a matter of minutes or even seconds. It is very easy to become swept away in the excitement and to feel very good about our achievements. However, we need to remember at all times that what we are doing is very normal and natural and that each and every one of us has the ability to do this. We are all special in our own right and none of us, regardless of our ability, is better than another in the grand scheme of things. It is very easy to put ourselves high on a pedestal whilst looking down at others, something that we must avoid at all costs. If we choose to work with ego the animals that we communicate with will recognise it straight away. For some animals this can be very off putting. We need to remember the true reason why we want to communicate which for most is a heart-felt desire. Staying true to ourselves is without a doubt one of the most important things in any aspect of spiritual work.

The Authentic Self

In the navel area we have an energy centre often referred to as the Soul Self, Ancient Self or the 'Hara'. This part of us is our connection to our Authentic Self and our integrity.

There are three areas of the body where we can experience our feelings. The head, the heart and the soul self. The head is the part of us that we use to rationalise these feelings and do what feels sensible - our logical thinking. Our heart can give us a romantic view and cause us to throw caution to the wind. Whilst our Authentic Self gives us the feeling to know what is right in the grand scheme of things. The next time you experience an emotional feeling take time to feel where abouts in your body you are experiencing it. You may feel a butterfly like sensation or a tingling, or just a knowing as to where the answer is coming from. Animals feel our energy and know our thoughts. They are instantly drawn to and feel more comfortable working with people who are not afraid to answer to themselves and choose to work with what they know to be true, rather than those who choose to cloud their own judgment by their beliefs and negativity.

The human brain is in very complex and consists of two hemispheres:

Left Hemisphere

This acts as a tool for the conscious part of the mind. The left side of our brain deals with the day to day issues that we have and our logical thinking side such as: reading, bill paying and thinking through problems. Others include identity, grandeur, the sense of the terrific, defiance, display, perfection and speculation.

Right Hemisphere

This acts as a tool for the sub-conscious part of the mind. The right side of our brain deals with our creativeness, imagination, psychic ability and meditation. It is this part of the brain that is often used by some of the world's great artists, musicians and poets. It also deals with love for animals, children and home, self-love, dignity, sympathy, intuition, human nature and self-esteem.

MEDITATION

Meditation is the action of quietening the mind. Something we do not have nearly enough of in our modern society. When we are in a meditative state we become much more relaxed, as we switch over to the right side of our brain and our brainwaves begin to slow down. This allows us to become far more receptive to hearing, seeing and experiencing. Our brain is a muscle; when we choose not to use it fully it becomes lazy and less active. Meditation is often referred to as 'mind yoga', as it is a very gentle and gets the brain working again without any vigorous exercise or distraction.

The more we meditate, the easier it will become to find that quiet space in our mind. When we do this, our heart rate will slow down and our physical body will become far more relaxed. Whilst meditating, it is not unusual for people to keep being interrupted by unwanted thoughts - this will lessen in time.

Exercise

Turn off any telephones or alarms that may disturb you

Lie or sit comfortably making sure that you are nice and warm

Close your eyes and take a few deep breathes

Give yourself a few moments to relax and clear your mind

In your mind's eye picture a white canvas

Each time a picture appears on the canvas mentally send it away

Do this for 2 minutes a day then up to 5-10 minutes over the course of 2 weeks.

Training the Mind

During all of our waking and sleeping states there is an ongoing change of brainwaves. These depend on what we are focused on and experiencing at the time. With practice, it is possible to learn to train our brain to react and correspond to a desired state in order to control our own brain activity and therefore our focus and awareness. By learning to do this, with practice, it is possible to achieve heightened states of awareness and relaxation at will.

Brainwave States

Beta is the highest mental state. It is associated with alertness and focused concentration or when engaged in mental activities, such as conversation or playing sports.

The Beta brainwave state corresponds to the frequency range of 13Hz to 40Hz.

The Alpha brainwave state is slower than Beta and is associated with reflection and relaxed mental focus, contemplation and visualisation.

It is also used for accessing deeper levels of creativity.

The Alpha brainwave state corresponds to the frequency range of 8Hz to 12Hz.

The Theta brainwave state is associated with meditation and relaxation. It is also used during light sleep and dreaming, as well as creativity and stress relief. It has been shown that 30 minutes a day of residing in the Theta brainwave state dramatically improves our well-being and general health, as well as enabling the need for less sleep.

The Theta brainwave state corresponds to the frequency range of 4Hz to 8Hz.

Delta is the lowest frequency state and is associated with dreamless sleep. It is possible to train yourself to remain awake in this state during deeper levels of meditation and awareness.

The Delta brainwave state corresponds to the frequency range of 0Hz to 4Hz.

The Gamma brainwave state is the most rapid of all the states. We briefly reach the Gamma state whilst receiving of high level information when processing occurs and during episodes of precognition.

The Gamma brainwave state corresponds to the frequency range of 40Hz or above.

Binaural Beats

Binaural Beats were discovered by German born H W Dove. He discovered was that when two signals of different frequencies are presented separately - that is one to each ear - it is possible that the brain will detect the phase variation between them. This then causes the brain to try and reconcile the difference that it finds, the difference being the Binaural Beats.

Example

If a frequency of 100Hz is presented on one side and the frequency of 105Hz on the other, the brain will recognise the third frequency pulsing at 5Hz, which is the difference between the two frequencies.

A binaural beat will cause the brain to resonate with the frequency of the beat. This is termed 'Frequency Flowing Response'.

By listening to a binaural beat it is possible to guide your brain to use a specific brainwave frequency by using the frequency following response method. If we are listening to a binaural beat pulsing at a frequency of 5Hz, which is a low Theta frequency. We can trigger our brain to resonate at that 5Hz frequency. This will automatically introduce brainwaves within the Theta range. The same is true for listening to a binaural beat pulsing at other frequencies corresponding to other brainwave states.

Brain Synchronisation

When our left and right brain hemispheres start to resonate to a binaural beat in synchronisation, we refer to it as 'whole brain synchronisation'.

This comes about when various parts of the brain begin to work together and resonate at the same frequencies. This causes neural pathways to fire more rapidly to enable information to flow more easily.

The energy patterns and electrical activity that form a pattern in the brain then become more wide spread, instead of remaining confined to certain areas.

Dendritic Growth

Growth is encouraged by neural stimulation within the brain. Dendrites are the branch fibers that extend from the neuron / cell body. As these fibers increase, so does the surface area that is available to receive information. The more dendrites our brain contains, the more quickly and easily we can process information.

HOW WE RECEIVE INFORMATION

Information about the animal's thoughts, feelings, experiences and health are all held within the animal's electromagnetic energy field. This is often referred to as the 'Aura'. Each individual piece of information is stored in the form of vibrational frequencies within this field.

By subconsciously reading these frequencies we are able to gain valuable information that is needed in order to help the animal. This is usually achieved whilst we are working in the Theta brainwave state. This information is then passed from our subconscious to our conscious in way that we can understand.

There are three main ways in which this information

is received.

Clairaudience

This is the ability to translate the information from the frequencies into words that we can understand. This may come in the form of single words or whole sentences. What we hear is our own interpretation of what the animal is saying. During this we will also be able to pick up on the type of personality the animal has, by the way we are hearing them speak. Some animals may come across as quiet and saying very little, whilst others may be very talkative. Some people will hear the voice as if it were their own speaking, whilst others will translate the information in more of an individual way better suited to the animal.

The voice may come across as very obviously male or female. As we are reading the animals energy it can sometimes be confusing as to the animal's gender. It is possible for a male animal to come across as having a very feminine, gentle nature and vice versa. If the animal comes across as very annoyed, angry or arrogant, we can usually take this as a valuable sign that the animal has an emotional issue.

Some animals may be very talkative and be only too happy to share what they need to say. At other times you will find others less forth coming and needing more of a question based approach, in order that you may gain the information from them that is required.

Clairsentience

This is the ability to 'feel' what the animal is both saying and feeling. This can be useful in a variety of different ways. Firstly, by working with clairsentience we are able to feel the animal's emotions and how they feel about certain things. For those people that have a strong sense of clairsentience the feelings that they pick up from the animal can be as informative as if they were actually hearing them speak. That is to say that rather than hearing actual words, we feel a definite knowing or feeling of what the animal is saying and feeling.

Clairsentience is also extremely useful in assessing an animal's health, as this can allow us to feel within our own body any areas of physical discomfort the animal may be experiencing. During our work with clairsentience when we are feeling the animal's emotions, it is not unusual to become tearful and upset. At this point it is important to understand that these are the animal's feelings that we are experiencing, not our own, and that they will soon pass once the connection has come to an end.

Clairvoyance

This is the ability to 'see' what the animal is showing us, as well as being able to see the animal's energy and other such energy systems. This can be useful in a variety of different ways such as:

Being able to view blockages within the animal's energy systems.

Viewing land energies and other such systems that may well be causing the animal a problem.

Being able to view problems to do with the animal's equipment or tack.

Mentally viewing what looks like still photographs of the animal's past, or even what looks to be a mental video playing of an event in the animal's life.

This can be a valuable tool to use when we are unable to hear or understand what the animal is saying, as we are then able to ask them to show us what they mean.

There is currently a school of thought that brings into question whether we actually see with our mind or with our physical eyes. Tests have shown that when the mind 'sees' or imagines, we have the same chemical reactions within the brain as we would do when seeing with our eyes. This gives us a firm understanding of why meditation can seem so real for us and how it can bring about such amazing results. This also brings into question whether we do truly see with our eyes or with our mind. Many of you will have heard people say that they have seen something with their 'third' or 'minds' eye. This is an energy situated in the centre of the forehead that allows us to see with the mind and internally within in us. When we are working with clairvoyance it is believed by many that this is where the energetic connection between what we are viewing and the actual viewing of it is made.

Clairambience

This is the ability to be able to taste or smell what the animal is experiencing or describing. Whist working with clairambience you may be able to taste or smell the food the animal is eating, or the food they are explaining to you that they like or dislike. This will sometimes be accompanied by the feeling or sensation of the temperature of the food.

During your connection with the animal you may also experience other smells or tastes that they wish you to experience within their environment, such as perfume, worn by the owner, or hold-house chemicals that are bothering them. Clairambience can also be a valuable tool during body scanning. It may be that you mentally experience the smell or taste coming from an animal due to a medical problem such as an infection or a stomach disorder.

THE ANIMAL AND HUMAN LINK

Within all relationships we encounter in our lifetime there are valuable lessons to be learnt. We may find that we are faced with an argumentative parent or partner, and within this kind of relationship our lesson maybe one of mastering the art of understanding, acknowledging and eventually accepting the ways of others by complementing their own deficiencies, and they ours. In the same way we also have valuable lessons to learn from our animals.

They can come into our lives for a variety of different reasons:

To teach us about ourselves as their problems may well resemble our own.

To mirror our behaviour by showing us how we are truly behaving and feeling.

To teach us how to love unconditionally, as animals pose no true treat to our feelings.

To enable us to feel at ease within a relationship when we have problems relating to other people.

To fulfill a karmic debt.

Looking at it from this perspective, animal / human relationships are just as important as our relationships with people. Studying how someone treats an animal and whether this is done with compassion, can give an insight into how that person relates to others. How they treat animals is a valuable clue to how they may treat other human beings. Studies have shown that children who abuse small animals are far more likely to grow up to commit violent crimes towards people, than those who have a love for animals at a young age.

What We Know To Be True

Anyone who has felt love for animal and a special bond or connection when in their presence, will come to realise what an important role animals play in our lives. Not just in the larger scheme of things, but also in each of our individual lives. In truth, when we come to understand what an animal truly is, rather than just what we perceive as, we come to a much deeper understanding of their true nature and the very point of their existence. Animals like ourselves are not just made of flesh and blood, but also of intricate energetic systems and many different levels of consciousness. There are some religions in the world that have denied the existence of the animal soul. If we choose to accept that the soul, or 'psyche' as it is often referred to, is part of the consciousness, or indeed its whole - then to deny the animals' soul existence would surely cause us to be in denial of an animal's ability to feel, express it's self or to even mentally exist. Looking at it from a logical point of view it is easy to see that this is not the case and that like ourselves, animals are more than just the physical bodies that many people still view them as.

How We Change

When this new realisation has come about it can open our eyes wide open to how we view the whole form of life and our interpretation of it. What is life? What is it all about? When we start to question the reason behind everything instead of taking as truth what we read, or what we are told, then we have set ourselves truly on the path of exploring not only ourselves, but also everything that is alive and in existence. Once we are on this path we have the opportunity to learn and grow. To realise our own beliefs through our personal experience, rather than to follow anyone chosen leader, or to adhere to the dogma of any one doctrine.

Pure Clarity

We will never find a more clear or truthful understanding to fuel our beliefs than through our individual experience of a situation, be it of a physical or spiritual nature. These times of sudden realisation are often referred to as 'light bulb moments', as they can often quite literally feel like someone has switched a light on for you. When we receive such feelings of clarity we can take it as a valuable sign that we are indeed moving forward with our way of thinking, how we view the world, and everything that exists in it.

Going With Feel

As our intuition heightens and our sense of self-belief comes to the forefront, we learn to trust and believe in ourselves and what we have come to understand and know to be true. We may be told something or read something that may well not sit comfortably with us, or resonate with us. We often term this as a 'gut feeling' when we experience it. We should listen to ourselves and take the appropriate steps as gut intuition can sometimes quite literally save our life!

Selfless Love

Partly due to the ego and much of our believed self-importance it is common for selfishness to become an over inflated part of us. Within the ego everything we can be - from selfish to loving - has a part to play and every right to be there. Within every negative attribute we have a positive. When we form this balance between the two we help to level our way of thinking.

Example

Our selfishness may be of service to us when people are applying unnecessary pressure to us through their own selfishness. Through our selfishness, or rather our 'need' for our own time, that may be viewed as selfishness. We find the courage to say 'no' and herein lies the positive attribute in the selfish attribute.

Example

In the case of a human / animal relationship there will sadly come a time when it is right for the animal to leave the physical plane. For many of us it is a sad time. These feelings of sadness that our animal will be physically leaving us can be overwhelming. Many people try and hold on to their animals and keep them with them for longer, by allowing them to undergo invasive operations or to be given a course of drugs that are not in the animal's best interests. When there is no hope and the animal is truly suffering, be it mentally or physically, we then have the option of stepping in and saying 'enough is enough' and allowing our animal to pass with dignity and love. Knowing that our decision was made through true love and understanding for the animal, rather than our own selfish desire to keep them with us. This gives much meaning to the phase 'sometimes love means letting go'.

WHAT ANIMALS KNOW

Animals do not have such an active ego, nor do they carry out judgments in the same way as we do. They have a much more simplistic way of viewing things. By simplistic I am referring to their non-complicated way of viewing things and their ability to see things as they truly are, rather than any implication of lesser intelligence on their part. From an emotional point of view, they can sometimes have a problem with rationalisation as indeed we all can. But in general their thoughts about the on-going cycle of life are much closer to the truth than many of us would assume. Whilst their past experiences can play a very relevant part in their present, they live very much in the now. Instead they choose to live without critical judgment of others, preferring to see others for what and who they really are, with a true focus on what they know to be important rather than wasting valuable energy on things that don't really matter. We can learn a lot from an animal's way of thinking when we choose to 'hear' them, rather than just 'listening' to what we expect to hear from them.

How the Animal Receives Information

The way that an animal receives information is slightly different from our own. The information comes to them more in a 'feeling' type way. We still send the information in the same way as we receive it, using pictures, words and feelings, but it's more the feeling and intention behind the information we send that the animal is better able to understand. The clearer we are in both our thought and intention, the clearer the information will be for the animal to understand.

How Animals React To Request

Now that we can understand how an animal receives information during telepathic communication, we can see why it isn't always the case that an animal will carry out an act that is requested. Any request the animal receives comes by way of a feeling of the need to do something, or that something has changed that may need reacting to. The animal may not be aware that the request (or feeling) has come from yourself or another person. Once the animal has received the feeling, they then have to make a conscious decision on whether to act upon the feeling or to ignore it.

Example

We can send a message to a horse that we wish it to walk forwards whilst giving it no physical cues. If the information is sent in clear enough detail to the horse so that it receives it, it will then get a feeling of needing to step forwards. If the horse can see no beneficial reason for moving forwards then chances are it will decide not to.

Animal/Human Psychology

Animal / human relationships, as well as playing a vital role in our growth, can also tell us a lot about ourselves. It is still commonplace for humans to see themselves higher up the evolutionary and intelligence ladder. Some of the reasoning behind this is due to the animal not being able to (as we see it) communicate as clearly as we do. Within each species there is a clear understanding of what each other are saying, from the noises they make, to their body language, eye contact and sharing of thoughts. Just because we sometimes have trouble understanding what animals are saying it doesn't mean that they aren't communicating just as clearly as we are.

Animals have no need for such complex

technologies as we use, no need for telephones or computers, as their way of long distance communication is far less complex and much more natural.

100th Monkey Syndrome

Japanese monkeys have been observed in the wild for 30 years on the island of Koshima. In 1952 scientists started to feed the monkeys with sweet potatoes that had been dropped in sand. Whilst the monkeys liked the taste of the raw sweet potatoes, they disliked the taste of the dirt and sand surrounding them.

Scientists observed that an 18 month old monkey, named Imo, found that she was able to solve this problem by washing the potatoes in a stream. She was observed doing this by other monkeys, thereby teaching her peers and family to wash their potatoes.

Over a period of time this was picked up by other monkeys and during 1952 through to 1958 scientists observed even young monkeys learning to wash their sweet potatoes. It was noted that older monkeys only learnt to do this through imitating and watching the younger monkeys who did this in their tribe. Consequently, it was found that some of the older monkeys still ate the dirty sweet potatoes.

In the Autumn of 1958 when a certain number of

the monkeys were washing their potatoes (for arguments sake the number of monkeys being 99), then later that day the 100th monkey also learnt and started to wash them. By the late evening, practically all the monkeys in the tribe were washing them, as if the energy brought about by the realisation of the 100th monkey has caused some sort of ideological breakthrough.

The most surprising thing the scientists witnessed was that the monkey's habit of washing the sweet potatoes suddenly started to show itself overseas. It was observed that colonies of other monkeys on islands and a mainland troop from Takasakiyama then began to wash theirs too. Scientists then came up with the theory that when a number of animals or people come to a certain awareness, this may well be communicated at vast distances through telepathy (mind to mind).

The understanding being that if only a limited number of people understand something of importance and the '100th monkey' (we use 100th as the exact number is not known or may vary) does not recognise this, the information cannot be spread in this way so it then remains the conscious property and understanding of the original people.

This example would then beg the question that if a large enough number of us were to come to a realisation of interspecies communication being a reality, over a period of time, the energy of that realisation would spread throughout the world and make it an active part of our lives. If this were to happen, then it would have a huge impact on the way that many of us choose to view and respect all living things in existence on our planet. This would in turn challenge us to readdress many of our beliefs and how we treat one another, as well as all living species. What a nice thought!

'Anthropomorphism' is a word that many of you will be familiar with. It basically means the assigning of human emotions to an animal - but do we actually assign human feelings to animals? - Or rather are we just understanding that animals do have emotions in just the same way as we do?

We only have to look at the physical signals and behaviour of animals to see that they experience exactly the same emotions we do.

Examples

A mare that protests and becomes distressed when her foal is removed for weaning - showing a maternal bond and sadness at that bond being broken.

A mare who grieves for her still born foal until such a time comes that she can come to an acceptance of its passing and covers it with straw as her final goodbye.

A dog that pines at the death of an owner shows its upset and distress at the absence of that much-loved owner.

A loyal dog that spends days, or even weeks next to its dead owner until someone comes and finds them.

A cat that is timid after being abused shows fear and lack of trust living in the fear that it could happen again.

A cat that leaves home because it can't cope with the atmosphere of sadness or anger that is constantly present in its home environment.

Animals appear to have not only all of the emotions we experience such as: grief, love, fear and resentment, but their way of thinking is without a doubt just as complicated and in-depth as our own. Not forgetting that animals also have all of the same Neuropeptides (emotional chemicals), not only in their brain, but also in their digestive tract, as humans do.

Example

Pearl is a 14-year-old horse. She has been with her owner Julie for the past 8 years. She has never shown any signs of ongoing stress or behaviour problems until the breakdown in relations between her owner and her owner's husband, at which time the husband left and no longer visited Pearl.

At this time Pearl became agitated and unsettled and would no longer be co-operative with her owner during handling or ridden work. This had been going on for around 18 months since the separation.

Pearl explains that she hates her owner because she made her 'dad' leave. (It is important to understand that as we are interpreting what Pearl is saying, that she views the husband as dad as he was the main male in her life who cared for her, and who she viewed as older. The same way that we may view an older male who cares for us as an 'uncle', even though they are not.)

Straight away, from how Pearl is speaking, we can see that she views her owner and her owner's husband as 'parents', as in those who care for her and her being in need of their nurturing. She sees herself as their child. So Pearl is angry with her 'mum' for making her 'dad' leave and breaking up the family unit and her security.

Further talks with Pearl start to show up a picture of self-blame when viewed from another perspective. In similar human situations it is often a mislaid blame that is focused towards the mother. In situations such as these, it is not uncommon that the child feels it is their fault that 'dad' didn't love or care for them enough so left them. Unable to cope with these emotions the only way that the child can cope with this is to project the blame elsewhere, thereby taking the emphasis off of themselves.

This was indeed the case for Pearl. Deep down she felt that her 'dad' had left because he had not loved her enough to stay, or because of something she had done or thought she should have done. Once getting to the bottom of how Pearl is viewing the situation, it can be explained to her that she isn't to blame and help her understand what was truly behind it. Once this has been done the resentment towards her 'mum' subsides (As Pearl now sees her mum wasn't to blame, but even more importantly that she wasn't either.) So Pearl's behaviour towards her 'mum' recedes and things go back to how they used to be once the realisation has been gained.

Another way to view 'behaviour' from an animal rather than seeing it as a behaviour problem, is to see it for what it is - an animal with a problem. Like children, animals develop behaviour problems as a way of showing something isn't right or comfortable for them.

Example

A dog that bites strangers: It may well be that the dog has been abused by people in the past and when meeting strangers they feel vulnerable.

A horse that wind sucks (The action of opening the mouth and biting on a stable door or fence post whilst sucking in air.) maybe displaying signs of stomach discomfort / hunger or frustration.

A cat that is shut in a house that obsessively scratches furniture and goes to the toilet on the carpet, may well be showing stress at being kept in.

Within all of these examples we can see that the reason for such behaviour is due to an underlying problem and that the animal isn't using the behaviour to cause a problem. They are simply playing out their distress at the situation they find themselves in. Therefore, should these behaviours truly be classed as 'bad' behaviour?

When asking an animal about its behaviour problem, it is important to first view the question from the animal's point of view. Is the behaviour a problem to the animal? If the answer is 'no' then it is unlikely that the animal will understand what you mean by their 'behaviour problem'. In such cases it is often clearer to explain the behaviour that you are referring to, and ask the animal why they feel the need to behave this way, rather than to label the behaviour as a problem as this could lead to confusion.

It is also often the case that like ourselves, animals can display upset through behaviour caused by a deeper subconscious memory or belief, that they are not consciously aware of. Sometimes this can lead to irrational fears, ideas or even phobias. Sometimes the cause of such things can be rooted in the animal's earlier years, or even in their past lives. The memories of which have stayed with them on a subconscious level.

Our own behaviour and outlook can have a huge impact on an animal's behaviour and their way of thinking.

When Animals Lie

As animals think and feel in very much the same way as we do. They too can lie - both consciously and subconsciously in a very similar way.

Consciously

This can happen when an animal is scared, ashamed or embarrassed to tell us something that they feel maybe used against them, or puts them in a vulnerable position. It may lead us away from an issue or line of enquiry that they do not wish to have pursued. By lying, they can lead us away from the truth, thereby protecting themselves and possibly others.

Subconsciously

This type of lying can be much harder to assess, as often even the animal isn't aware of it. It is usually used as a distraction to lead us (and often themselves) away from a very traumatic memory.

Example

We may ask an animal if it is happy. It then assures us that it is. It may be that the animal in question is in fact unhappy, but doesn't want to acknowledge the fact as if it does, it then has to deal with the reason for the unhappiness. The animal consciously convinces itself that is happy and that all is well as a way of self-guarding itself.

Most, if not all cases of subconscious lying, are a way of protecting ourselves. Our subconscious thinks that it is doing us a favor by hiding away details and feelings that may well bring about a negative effect and upset. Unfortunately, when this happens, the negative vibration held within the energy field when allowed to stay for a long period of time, can start to distort the energy systems - eventually often leading to physical illness.

There are several ways that we can spot subconscious lying in animals. Sometimes it might be something as simple as a contradiction an animal makes during its communication that it later retracts or tries to 'tidy over' when asked about it. It may be that you experience a 'gut feeling', or have a physical reaction, such as being covered in goose bumps or experience shivers down your spine. All of which should be taken as a sign that something isn't right within the conversation. Although it should be noted that shivers down the spine and goose bumps can also be associated with confirmation of what is being said. These physical cues are created by the nervous system reacting to information. Over time, if you experience these feelings, you will learn to understand their meaning by assessing the information that is being received at the time they occur.

When you have learnt to recognise a subconscious lie, question the animal gently about it, just as you would a person get them to look at the bigger picture as to how they feel about the situation they have been talking about. Ask them to analyse it in a more open manner to see if they can understand the reason for it. If you are able to do this together, it might well be that you can get to the reasoning behind it and are able to deal with the issue at hand.

The Reluctant Animal

Like people some animals are more approachable than others and some are more willing to talk. How open to talking the animal is will very much depend on its personality. Some will be very talkative and chat away none stop hardly pausing for breath, whilst others will be less willing to comply and will work much better with an asking them questions basis. Now and again you may come across an animal that isn't willing to talk which can be not only frustrating, but can also knock your confidence. Some animals can be very much like children in the way that they like to receive attention. An animal that likes having people take notice of it and thrives on the attention it can bring itself, may well not speak, as it is enjoying the coaxing it is receiving. In such cases, once the animal feels it has received enough attention, it will usually then choose to connect with you, or you may tell them you are disconnecting, and then they suddenly choose to engage with you.

Animals can also recognise our energy the moment we connect with them. If we are not in a very pleasant mood, or if we are feeling rushed or worried the animal may well pick up on this and feel that our energy is not a nice one to connect to. This can often be physically witnessed by the way that animals are drawn to certain people whilst they try and steer clear of or ignore others.

Some animals when they are not well practiced in communicating can sometimes find it hard to stay connected and focused. This can sometimes be the case for very young animals as well. In such cases it is often useful to communicate with an animal friend of theirs, who is often able to pass on the information on their behalf. Also, remaining patient is advisable. If they feel you are trying to hurry them it can bring them stress.

Another reason for an animal being reluctant to communicate is that by reading your energy when you connect to them, they are able to see that you are capable of seeing their true self. Like us, many animals choose to wear a mask falsely showing the world who they want to be seen as. This doesn't have to mean that they are bad in any way, just that they may have a lack of confidence in themselves that they do not wish you to see through.

When coming up against a reluctant animal that you have a problem communicating with, there are several different ways of trying to get them to engage in conversation with you. You can try asking them questions so if they are not very talkative, you can at least gain the information required in order to help them, or secondly, you can ask them what they would like to talk about - thereby leaving the door wide open and the ball in their court.

Approaching the Animal

As we have already discussed, the moment we choose to connect to animal they are aware of our energy. In order that we make ourselves as inviting as possible for the communication to take place, it is important that we are calm and focused. We need approach the situation by understanding how it feels to the animal.

How do you feel when you meet a stranger and they start to talk to you?

Do you feel nervous, surprised or shocked?

Are you able to decide at that moment whether or not you feel comfortable in this person's presence and talking to them?

This is exactly how it is for the animal. When we are happy and we are enjoying the situation, the animal will pick up on a friendly energy that you are exhibiting. In most cases they will comfortable enough to talk with you. If you are feeling under the weather, or you are in a negative frame of mind, it is sometimes better to wait until it passes in order that your energy feels friendly.

HOW TO INTERPRET

Information can come in many different forms including smells, pictures (both moving and still), or words and feelings. We all have our own unique way of communicating and how we interpret the information received. When the information comes in a fragmented manner, it can quite literally feel like we are having to put together the pieces of a jigsaw puzzle. An animal may say that it 'feels' like its leg is broken. The emphasis here is then on the word 'feel'. Chances are the animal's leg is not broken. It is just that it uses this description as a way of helping us to understand the kind of pain, or discomfort that is being experienced. When we see things such as colours, if we do not see as clearly as we do with our eyes, we can easily confuse them, such as dark brown and black, which can sometimes be confusing.

Sometimes an animal may say something that we don't understand. When this happens, try asking the animal to repeat it. If the information is correct, even though not understood, or if it holds major importance, it maybe that it is accompanied by a physical sensation such as goose bumps or shivers, or even just an inner sense of knowing.

A dog that has an allergy to carpet shampoo may refer to the green lawn in the house that can be interpreted as the carpet.

When communicating with animals it is not unusual for them to bring up strange information. They may talk about a past life when they were another animal, or even a human and what happened to them at this time. Hear them out as this information is relevant to their healing. You will need to understand what happened to them, or what emotional or physical scars that life time left them with, in order to aid them in moving forwards in the here and now.

From a medical point of view, we can choose mental tools with which to work that can aid us in our interpretation. When viewing an animal's joint we can choose to mentally view it as a strong beefy bone, or as a splintering chicken bone - depending on how that joint is physically, in order to access what state of repair it is in. With areas of soreness or inflammation, it is possible to use a 'colour chart' ranging from healthy tissue colour - through to red and then purple and brown. This can give us a clear insight into the state of the area. For example: red may be an area of inflammation or infection, or deep purple or brown may show us dead flesh or dried blood in that area - whilst grey may represent toxins.

The key to communicating is to take on board everything that the animal says and to analyse it in depth afterwards if you can't make out the meaning of something at the time. Of course, anything we don't understand we can easily question the animal about in more depth. When we have limitations in our understanding it can come about due to a lack of terms of reference from our subconscious memory banks, especially from a medical point of view. The more knowledge we have about Anatomy, Holistic Medicine, Therapies, Allopathic Medicine and the Spiritual World - the more easily we will be able to interpret the information in a clear manner, so that it makes more sense to us.

When Something Doesn't Feel Right

Sometimes during communication something won't feel quite right. It's not always what the animal says or how it says it - sometimes it might just be a gut feeling that we have. When experiencing what you recognise to be your gut feeling take it on board.

Gut feeling is a very strong intuitional tool to have and when used it can prove very useful. Question around the situation and play detective to see if you can get to the bottom of things. Often when something doesn't feel right it isn't!

Animal Emotions and Cellular Level

Cellular level vibration and emotions all carry a vibrational signature. It could be that an animal was eating at a roadside when it was hit by a car. As each cell of the body has its own unique intelligence separate from the brain, the cells of the body during this time will access the body to see what isn't normal for it at the time of trauma. It may well be that the cells recognise the food being eaten at the time as a being a foreign body. When this happens it may well be that the cells choose to recognise such foods as an allergen. If this is the case, it may be that in the future when the same food is eaten, the animal will have the physical symptoms of a food allergy or intolerance. In the same way if an animal has an accident that is emotionally traumatic for it, the emotional cellular memory of the incident can stop the injury from healing quickly, due to the energy of the cells being stuck in trauma shock.

As well as accidental trauma manifesting problems, so can pure emotional trauma. When the animal holds negative emotions within their energy field, the vibrational frequencies over time will distort the homeostasis of the physical body. This will usually lead to physical illness. For most, if not all illnesses, there may be both physical and emotional symptoms. By addressing the emotional discord through healing, we can help to heal the physical body too, by going straight to the route of the problem

Other Examples

Dogs or horses that mentally maintain their lameness as a way of avoiding being walked or ridden. It sounds odd, but if not as uncommon as you would think.

Animals who don't want to get well, as illness either serves them a purpose (attention,) or they feel that they don't deserve to be well.

Female animals that don't fall pregnant because they are scared, maybe from when they have experienced a bad time during their own birth, or a trauma whilst giving birth previously.

Non-Violent Communication and Training Methods

There are no end of training methods available to use, but are all such methods in the animals' best interests? In recent years there has been a resurrection in Natural Horsemanship training methods and more termed natural approaches towards the training of other species. On first inspection of many such named methods, the animal appears to understand what is being said and physical results are seen. But what is the animal experiencing and thinking?

In many forms of training methods the animal is put in a situation where it has a limited choice of how to react. In some cases when the desired affect is not seen, gadgets are applied that cause tension or pressure to the animal - either mentally or physically. If the animal has no intention of allowing physical discomfort to come into play, they are given little choice as to whether or not to comply. With these kinds of training methods there is always an implied 'if you don't do what I ask, I will do this to you'. Regardless of whether or not the implied threat is carried through or not - it is still a threat. This could well be considered violent communication. There are many gadgets to help 'control' behaviour that are available on the market.

These include nut cracker throat collars used to stop a horse wind sucking (gulping air), head collars that cause tension over the nose when pressure is applied to the lead rope, or even head collars with metal studs around the headpiece of the collar that runs across the top of the head behind the ears.

Many of these gadgets will bring about the desired

affect - but is it for the right reason?

Much is the same with many dog-training methods where choke chains, spiked collars, citrus squirting collars (used for barking) or electric shock collars are used. Such things stop the animal's behaviour by causing discomfort, whilst not taking into consideration why the animal feels the need to exhibit such a behaviour in the first place.

Through communication we can ask the animal why they feel the need to behave in such a way. This then enables us to address the problem in a kind and sympathetic manner.

When training animals or seeking a new training method, try to view the psychology of it through the animal's eyes.

How would it make them feel?

Does it give them time to think?

Why is it working?

Would you consider it violent (A threat being implied or carried out) or is it non- violent, where the animal will see a reward for good behaviour and be able to make safe choices?

When animals are put in a situation where they can think things through and see a reason why the new improved behaviour would be of benefit to them, you are much more likely to have a willing training partner. The main thing is never lose sight of why they display such behaviour in the first place. What we perceive as a behaviour problem may not be viewed as such by the animal. Looking at their environmental situation and our own behaviour can easily rectify many everyday behaviour problems shown by our pets.

CONDUCTING A SESSION

Firstly, before we begin to communicate we must prepare ourselves both mentally and physically. We must decide whether or not we intend to communicate in person with the animal physically present, or through distance communication. Both will bring about the same results, but other things also need to be taken into consideration.

If you are communicating with an animal that is likely to constantly nudge you, you may find yourself distracted. Or if you are in a field or a stable in the middle of the winter and are cold, you might find that again that you have problems concentrating. Other things such as time spent travelling also need to be weighed up.

Whether you choose to be in the physical presence

of the animal in question or not, the process is basically the same. There are several ways we can choose to conduct the session. It maybe that you decide to let the animal run the session and do all the talking. The problem you may find if you intend to work this way is that the animal might not be particularly communicative or that the information the owner is looking for may not be forthcoming. By asking the animal what they wish to say, we can leave the doors open for anything we might otherwise miss hearing. This works rather well when followed by a question and answer type session, where we ask the animal things the owner wishes to know about so that we can pass on the answers to them.

In Person

Sit or stand with the animal that you wish to communicate with. You may find that you wish to touch them in order to connect with their energy more easily.

Close your eyes and take a few deep breaths.

Allow your energy to flow outwards and towards the animal, with the intention that they will feel it and choose to connect with you.

Then relax as the information comes to you in the form of words, pictures and feelings.

When you feel the need to ask a question, phrase it in a positive way so that if it is received in a fragmented manner, no vibration of any negative words such as 'hurt' or 'danger' will be experienced by them.

Once the communication has come to an end, remember to thank the animal for communicating with you.

Distance Communication

Sit or lie comfortably in a warm room without any distractions such as telephones or radios.

Close your eyes and picture the animals face looking at you as if they need to tell you something.

Send out the energy and intent that you are open and willing to hear them.

Alternatively, you might find it easier to close your eyes and picture the room you are in, as you watch them mentally enter the room and sit beside you. Again, remember to phrase the information you are sending them in a positive way and thank them again once the session has come to a close.

All Thought Is Energy

Now that we are ready to start to communicate with

our animals, we need to understand the energetic dynamics behind it.

Every thought we have, every word we speak and every single intention that we have, carries a vibrational signature. When intention is put behind a word it can have a positive or negative affect. This will depend on the type of word it is, and the expression behind it. The words we send out and receive when communicating aren't so much what the animal receives from us. It is more the energetic dynamic behind the spoken word and what it means. We can understand this by accessing how we feel when people speak to us. Not only by the words they use, but also by how those words make us feel when used with intent and emotion.

Example

If someone tells us that they 'hate' us, it will cause us a very different feeling to when someone tells us that they 'love' us.

So when we are communicating, in order to help the animal to feel as comfortable as possible, we need to phrase our thoughts and words in a positive way.

'Nothing will hurt you in your stable. No one will ever hit you again when you are in there'.

The above statement when received in a fragmented

manner by the animal can bring about negativity due to these parts: Hurt you and hit you.

We can adjust the statement to: 'You will always be safe in your stable and will always feel comfortable with people in there'.

This will give the statement an overall positive feeling.

Negativity, or the type of negativity can have a bigger impact on some animals than others. For some animals emotional discord is far more distressing than physical disharmony and vice versa. What one animal might call a 'smack', another animal might see as a 'beating'. In the same way, two animals who have had their owner's throw a food bowl at them in temper, may view it in a different way due to the intent behind it. One may view it as distressing and see the frustration behind it and feel scared. Whilst another may feel their human's emotions and know that they aren't angry at them. They are frustrated and upset about something else, so that the animal knows that this display is not aimed at them personally. The outcome due to feeling the emotion and intent of throwing of the food bowl at them, can therefore bring about a different feeling about the situation and so a totally different outcome as to how they feel and view it emotionally.

The moment we choose or intend to connect with an animal, they know how we are feeling at that time. This will have an influence on our energy and the way in which the animal interprets it. If we are feeling under the weather, negative, angry or in any other way not positive. We are not feeling as comfortable to connect with as we could do, and the animal may not be so willing to communicate with us. By assessing our own feelings and dispelling with any negative thoughts we are holding onto, we make ourselves far more approachable and comfortable to connect with. At this time we also need to assess our intention and our integrity.

What is our intention?

Are we purely in this job for the money?

Or because if we can find out about the animal's physical illness we might be able to save ourselves from an expensive veterinary diagnosis?

That we want to impress people?

Or is it that we genuinely have a heartfelt desire to help?

Whatever your intention behind your communication - the animals will know the moment that you connect with them. If your intentions aren't of the highest integrity, the communication my lack in information the animal may otherwise have passed on.

When we choose to communicate for the wrong reasons, it may well be that whilst the animal is happy to talk with us about day to day issues and about medical problems. It may not feel comfortable enough to discuss deep emotional issues, even though these may well be the underlying problem behind all of its other problems in the first place

Taking a Case Study

Before we start our case study, we must first decide which way we would like to work. This can either be with a question and answer type approach, or we may decide that we just want to see what the animal has to say for themselves.

It might also be a good idea to discuss which type of approach the animal's person feels would be more beneficial.

At the beginning of a communication it is always a good idea to ask the animal's owner if they would like you to briefly explain animal communication and how it works, so that they can gain a better understanding of what is likely to happen.

Any previous information that the owner offers is useful, but not always necessary. Although, if information is offered, it may help us fit pieces of the jigsaw puzzle together and also to help us assess how best to phrase our questions.

Recording

It is always useful to keep a written record of any communication to refer back to at a later date. This might be so that over time we can assess how the animal is progressing, or simply so that we don't forget any important pieces of information that we receive. By making a carbon copy of the communication or a photocopy, we then have both a copy for our-self, and also one for the owner. Emailing it as a Word Document is also a good idea, as we can then pass one copy on and file another for our own records.

Making notes whilst communicating can be very difficult and distracting. If you have someone with you whilst you are communicating, ask them if they will do the writing for you so that you can give the communication your undivided attention.

It is always advisable that whenever possible, you fill out as much of the communication sheet as you can, so that you have all of the information needed before hand. The actual communication information and any additional information can then be added during, or after the communication has taken place.

Example

Owners Name

Address

Telephone Number

Email Address

Date of Communication

Animals Name

Species

Breed

Colour

Age

Any known problems

Any known illnesses

Any previous information given by owner

Example Questions

How does he feel emotionally?

How does he feel physically?

Is he in any pain?

Does he feel his food is right for him?

How does he feel about our relationship?

How does he feel about the other dogs and cats in the house?

Does he enjoy his training?

Is there anything he needs to tell me?

Does he know it is safe to voice his concerns?

Does he feel he has recovered alright after his operation?

Some people also find that the owner is a useful link for them, in order that they can tune in to the animal more successfully. You may also choose to use what we refer to as a 'witness'. This is something that has a connection to the animal such as a photograph of the animal, or a piece of the animal's hair. Some people feel that the witness helps them to establish a better or easier first connection with the animal.

Audio recording is more often used as the communicator's record of the communication. Sometimes you might find that this your preferred way of working and you make a copy of the recording for the animal's owner. The problem with verbally recording a communication is that there may be long gaps within it when your focus is on the communication with the animal. You may become distracted by sorting out the words and phases you need in order to get the information across.

If you do decide to use the verbal form of recording for you communication, you first need to decide what format it will take.

Do you intend to write down contact details first, or record it at the time?

Are you just communicating with the animal and repeating its words in the same format as they come to you?

Are you going to first record the question and then communicate with the animal - followed by recording the answer?

An alternative and easier approach to this is to still have a written record of all the questions that are to be asked, then just record all the answers as they come. If this is your preferred way of working, then any CD should be marked with the animal's and owner's name, as well as the date of the communication and be kept with a written record of the questions that have been asked.

When Animals Don't Want To Well

It is a sad fact that many animals remain in ill health, be that of a physical or emotional nature - through their own making. It maybe that the animal in question has a low self-esteem and for whatever reason feels they do not deserve the special attention and treatment required. The low self-esteem may have come from many years of neglect and not experiencing a loving owner, or from years of being told or made to feel that they are useless and unworthy. When we come across a situation like this, it is our job to explain to them just how much they are loved, how much they are cared for, and to pass on information to the owner about how they can aid them further. This may well be in the form of Hands on Healing, or some form of other therapy, but reassurance goes a long, long way.

Munchausen By Proxy

This is a psychological illness whereby people use their animal's distress or illness to gain attention for themselves. It may also show in the form of putting their animal on 'display'.

The physical form of the illness is easier to identify as it often presents obvious physical symptoms. This can range between something such as someone dying their poodle pink, to physically causing harm to their animals by wounding them or feeding them food or medicines that they know to be harmful.

The energetic form of the illness usually involves a subconscious desire on the side of the owner to maintain their animal's illness. This is done on an energetic level by constantly draining them of their energy in a bid to keep them weak. In this case it is unlikely that the owner will be aware of what they are doing.

So What Is Munchausen By Proxy?

Munchausen by Proxy is a psychological illness whereby the sufferer uses their animal (or child) to gain attention for themselves. Usually the person in question will have something missing from their life that is unfulfilled. Often this is through not receiving attention from other people. By physically or energetically (subconsciously) maintaining their animal's illness, they gain people's pity and understanding, that then aids them to feel better. Many people who have the disorder on a physical level are aware that they are doing it, though they may not always be sure of the reasoning behind it. People who do it on an energetic (subconscious) level are usually - though not always unaware.

Similarly, people can drain an animal of their energy as a way of boosting their own, rather than choosing to channel it from elsewhere.

Symptoms

The owner who chooses not to get medical attention the animal needs.

A person who pushes their animal out in front of them, using them to hide behind. By people noticing the animal, the owner will then be noticed.

An owner who continuously talks about their animal to the point that they lose friends as there is no other topic of conversation.

People who take their animal from vet to vet, from therapist to therapist and then claim that no one has been able to help them, but they know that you are 'the one' who can. Usually this will involve the changing of many vets and therapists over short period of time, so that the relevant people aren't able to have long enough to treat the animal with any chance of success.

The owner who says that money is no issue and then spins a very long tale about how much they love their animal, how much money they have spent on them, with no improvement seen. This may even be over a span of years.

The owner who repeatedly telephones you any time during the night or day, trying to gain as much sympathy from you as they can, with their woeful stories of how things aren't improving with their pet.

Obviously, some of these symptoms can be totally genuine with no cases of Munchausen behind them, but more often than not, when three or more of these symptoms are shown, there will be an element of the problem existing.

When someone is harming their animal in such a way, it can be very distressing for us as an outsider looking in. We can feel helpless to do anything. In the case of physical harm being caused we can notify the relevant authorities, but with the energetic form of this mental illness there is a lot less that we can do to help. That is unless the animal's owner chooses to recognize that they have an illness.

In order to stop the animal's owner from draining us in the same way, we need to step back a little and approach the whole situation in a professional manner, so that we don't find ourselves caught up in the owner's self-made drama. It can be very hard to help an animal in these circumstances, as on an energetic level much that we do to help will be counteracted by the owner. One thing that we can do is wrap the animal up in golden healing light to help keep them safe. Then we can explain to them that we understand about their situation, that we are always open and willing to listen whenever they need us.

BODY SCANNING

Body Scanning can be used for many different things. It can be used for looking for blockages and the state of the physical body, location of discomfort and stiffness, as well as looking at the make-up and disruptions of the animals' energy systems.

The Etheric Body is energetic in its make-up and consists purely of energy. It is made up of several different energy systems.

The Aura exists around the physical body. It has many different layers, the main ones being:

First Layer – The Physical Plane

This relates to the base chakra. It bridges the

connection between the energy body and the physical body.

Second Layer – Emotional Body

This relates to the sacral chakra. It is associated with the vibrations of inner feelings.

Third Layer – Mental Body

This relates to the solar plexus chakra. It is associated with the vibrations of the ego, mental thought processes and our thoughts.

Fourth Layer – Astral Body

This relates to the heart chakra. It is associated with our expressions of feeling on a mental, emotional and physical level.

Fifth Layer – Spiritual Plane

This is related to the throat chakra. It is our blueprint for the lower etheric body.

Sixth Layer – Celestial Body

This relates to the brow chakra. It is associated with our 'enlightenment'.

Seventh Layer – (Etheric) Casual Body

This relates to the crown chakra. It is associated with our connection to the Divine.

Eight Layer – Cosmic Plane

This is associated with to our past and future karma and is our link to the Akashic records.

Ninth Layer – Soul Body

This is associated with the connection between where we are now, and what we perceive as heaven.

Tenth Level – Integrative Body

This is associated with the connection between the physical and spiritual worlds. It is able to disconnect from the physical body to enter into the astral realms.

It is not unusual to find as many as 14 auric layers within the animal's aura - sometimes even more.

Chakras

These are energy vortices in the energy body of the animal. Animals have primary and secondary chakras. When the chakras are out of balance due to physical or emotional ailments, healing can help to restore the balance and aid repair.

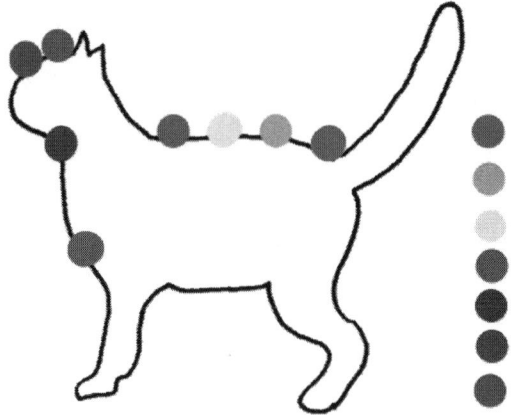

Meridians

These are energy pathways throughout the body some of which are linked to major organs. They are used in Chinese Medicine for Acupuncture and Acupressure treatments. There are 66 meridians in all. Only 14 of these meridians are commonly known of and used. Different meridians in the body carry slightly different energy. We will focus on the most commonly used meridians that are known to carry 'Chi' throughout the body. Each meridian has a partner meridian that it works in conjunction with and that it has connections to.

Jing Creative and Generative Energy

Chi Life Force Energy

Shen Spiritual Energy

Each type of these energies are made up of five elements:

Water Element Meridians

Bladder and kidney
Colour: Blue

Wood Element Meridians

Liver and gall bladder

Colour: Green

Fire Element Meridians

Heart and small intestine
Colour: Red

Earth Element Meridians

Stomach and spleen
Colour: Orange

Metal Element Meridians

Lung and Large intestine
Colour: Grey

The Conception Vessel and the Governing Vessel

Colour: Black or white

The Etheric Body is the blue print for the physical body. When parts of the energy system become blocked or disrupted, over time the imbalances can filter through to the physical body, often leading to ill health. By maintaining them in a healthy balance we can aid physical, mental and emotional well-being.

There are several ways that we can scan an animal.

We can choose to scan them physically or mentally, in person, at distance, or choose to scan the physical body or the energy systems.

Body Scanning In Person

When we are in the company of the animal that we are going to body scan we have several options. We can choose to hold our hands on or just above the animal, to see what physical sensations we pick up.

These may include:

Tingling

A knowing of where to place our hands and for how long

Electric shock type feelings

Heat or cold

It may even be that we can see energetic disruptions over certain parts of the body that may indicate an issue.

Just go with your intuition as to what needs to be done.

We can also choose to mentally scan the animal. Often closing our eyes helps us to focus, as when we have our eyes open we can revert back to the wide awake Beta brainwave state. Alternatively we can move our eyesight around the animal's physical body, taking note of any areas that we are drawn to.

If you find this difficult - relax a little more and don't try too hard.

Scanning Tack and Other Equipment

The same method we use for scanning the body and energy systems may also be used for scanning objects such as saddles, bits, collars etc.

As well as mentally associating the object with the animal and feeling which part if any maybe suspect. We can also mentally put the piece of equipment on the animal using our mind vision and check the fit. If the animal is showing any signs of discomfort around the areas that the equipment fits, try scanning the physical body and the equipment to see if the areas showing up correspond.

For example: A sore area on a horse's back and their saddle.

Symbolic Signs and Meanings

Due to how our mind chooses to interpret and also down to our own level of understanding, it may be that sometimes things might not come through as clearly as we would like. For instance, if we have a poor level of knowledge about the physical body it may be that we choose to interpret it in a symbolic manner.

Example

If we are viewing the animal's liver and find it to be unhealthy, we may see it as shriveled or as a different colour such as green or grey. This could be an indication of toxins or disease.

In time the symbols that are personal to you will be repeated when you come across the same problem over and over. It is very often just a case of putting pieces of the jigsaw together in order to decipher what they mean. The more you practice and the better knowledge you have of the physical body, energy systems and other therapies, the easier and clearer the information will be presented to you. If at any time you come across something that you don't understand, keep a mental note of it as well as writing it in the animal's records. Chances are, once you come across it for a second time, or have had more time to think, the meaning behind it will become apparent.

EARTH ENERGIES

Animals are very sensitive to energy and changes in energy. Often when they can feel energies that are new to them it can feel confusing. In some cases they are unable to understand whether they are positive or negative for them. In many cases this can bring about a feeling of uncertainty or even panic and avoidance.

The earth consists of many types of land energies. Many can be likened to charkas or meridians that exist in human and animal bodies. However, many other land energies exist, such as those given off by standing stones and old religious sites. Also, those given off from residual energies such as those left over from an old battle site or old slaughterhouse.

This can sometimes make animals react in strange

ways. Animals such as dogs and horses are most commonly affected due to covering more ground. Cats of course often cover large distances and may be affected. It is just that we aren't often there to witness their change in behaviour ourselves. Also, as they are free roaming, they are able to avoid these areas much more easily.

Symptoms of Land Energy Behaviour

Barking at seemingly nothing

Spinning in circles

Rearing (in the case of horses)

Reluctance to pass certain areas on a singular or repeated basis

Refusing to enter certain fields, gardens or buildings or certain areas of them

Animals that experience earth energies often describe them as causing sensations such as tingling, trickling, electric shocks, or just as a strange atmosphere. Some animals are able to see earth energies and may choose to describe them to you in the form of colours and pictures. This can help you to understand the type of energies that you are seeing.

When coming across an animal that appears nervous or is suffering from behaviour problems due to earth energies, it is advisable to help the owner to find someone who has knowledge of how to work with these energies. This maybe someone qualified in Geomancy or maybe a Crystal Therapist who can choose crystals to stop the animal feeling the sensations, or who can crystal grid the areas involved.

Spiritual Problems

Animals can suffer from spiritual problems in much the same way as humans do.

These can come in two different forms:

Disconnection from the Transpersonal Self

In such cases the animal may feel 'lost' and disconnected from itself. By not being fully mentally and spiritually integrated, animals can be open to psychological disorders such as Multiple Personality Syndrome and depression.

Outside Spiritual Influences

This can very much fall into the realm of spirits. Animals may be seen acting in strange ways, like running dangerously from apparently nothing in blind panic, or barking, or lunging viciously at something that can't be seen, although lesser symptoms maybe seen, such as, growling at what appears to be mid-air - to avoiding certain places. Animals that encounter such problems might tell of 'something' chasing them - something they can see, or changes in temperature whilst they are stationary in one place.

In such cases it is advisable to contact someone who works in the field of removing these types of energies. Some of these energies are only a problem when they are upsetting an animal. These could be energies such as another animal that has died but wants to stay close to them, or who had lived there previously and still sees the place as 'home'. Whilst not threatening in nature, if the animal is unable to understand what it is feeling, it may become a problem.

WORKING WITH OTHER THERAPISTS

As much as it is interesting and rewarding working with many kinds of therapies, if we choose to cover too many fields, we can spread ourselves too thinly. As you develop in your work you are likely to meet other Therapists and Healers that you feel drawn to. This can be very useful, not only from the point of view that you are able to pass work and clients to each other, but also that you can share your ideas and experiences.

Each one of us has our own unique way of working that will have a place to fill in the bigger picture. We all give off slightly different energies and what suits one animal may not suit another.

Therapies

Here is a list of commonly used therapies that you may well find useful to aid the animals that come into your care. All of these therapies can be worked with in either a 'text book' or an intuitive way, the latter often being the most beneficial to the animal. Many, but not all Therapists, have an element of energy work within their therapy depending on their own level of understanding and advancement.

Chiropractic

This therapy involves the gentle manipulation of the body to help realign the spinal column. Sometimes this can take several treatments as in order for the bones to stay in place, the muscles must be strong enough to hold them there. If an animal has been misaligned for a long period of time the muscles would have adapted to holding the body in this new way. It can take twenty-one days for the muscles to reform and be able to hold the body into its new and correct alignment.

Homoeopathy

The idea behind homeopathy is that when using it, we are treating 'like with like'. The dis-ease or illness held within the body will hold a certain vibrational signature unique to that illness, the idea being that by treating the body and energy systems with the 'same' vibration - the vibration is then cancelled out.

Like all therapies and medications that are energetic in nature, Homoeopathy should only be used by those who are very experienced and educated in its uses. Currently it is only legal for a suitably qualified Veterinary Surgeon, or the animal's owner to prescribe such remedies for an animal.

Herbalist

It is believed by some people that for each illness or dis-ease, there is a natural plant source to help combat or solve the problem. Each herb used has a medicinal property that when used correctly and in the right dosage, can help the body to correct itself, release toxins or provide itself with the nutrition needed. Herbs have been used for many thousands of years in Chinese Medicine with often amazing results.

Animals have an inbuilt intuition as to the healing ability of herbs. When left in a natural environment they will often be seen self-medicating. When we make herbs unavailable to animals within their everyday environment, we then of course take away the availability for them to self-medicate. In the case of grazing animals, pastures are best maintained naturally without the use of weed killers. Much of what we view as weeds is medication to our animals.

Example

Chamomile - Calming and soothing

Milk thistle - A good liver tonic

Dandelion - Helps support the urinary system

Plantain - High in nutrition

Spiritual Healing

This therapy involves the Healer channeling Chi (Life Force Energy) into the animal. This may be carried out by touching the animal, or by holding the hands slightly away from them. Energy is then channeled from the Universal Energy Source into the Healer and out of the palms of their hands towards the animal. The energy will then find its own way into the physical and energetic parts that it needs to reach. Spiritual Healing can also be carried out at distance in much the same way.

A more commonly known form of Hands on Healing is known as 'Reiki'. It is believed that the ability to heal, or channel healing energies is passed down from 'master' to student, through a series of 'attunements'. This of course alone does not make up for experience. It is advised that those who choose this path continue to learn about healing and the energy systems as a way of gaining as much understanding of it as they can.

Flower Remedies

Flower remedies are made by infusing certain flowers in spring or mineral water. Brandy is then added as a preservative. The flower infusion then imprints the remedy with the vibration of the flower. This can then be used to correct emotional imbalances. There are literally hundreds of flower remedies available, each suited to a different state of mind. The most commonly known are the Bach Flower Remedies.

Radionics

This therapy is sometimes used with what is termed 'The Black Box', or at other times used with dowsing. The idea is that the animal's energy systems are read and deciphered and any blockages or abnormalities are dealt with by sending the correct vibration signature to correct them. This therapy in past years was given little credit, but more recently it has become much more widely accepted. As with many other therapies, it can be used not only for correcting health problems, but also with maintaining good health and as a preventative. In recent years it has become commonly used in the competition horse world.

Behaviour Problems

An animal showing the signs of a behaviour problem can be viewed in two different ways:

Either as an animal with a behaviour problem, or an animal that has a problem that chooses to display that it is feeling unsettled. The latter being closer to the truth as an animal is unable to voice its concerns or problems in another way. This causes the negative feelings and emotions being experienced to tend to manifest in behaviour that we see as undesirable.

Possible Symptoms

Biting

Rearing

Bucking

Chewing (Themselves, others or furniture)

Noises (Growling, whimpering or barking)

Not coming when called

Kicking or striking

Weaving (Swaying the head from side to side whilst stepping from one foot to another)

Wind sucking (Gulping in air through the mouth)

There are many devices on the market that make all sorts of claims to stop such behaviours. But is this really the right way of going about it?

Is it in the best interests of the animal?

Some of the behaviours listed above release endorphins from the brain that can help calm the animal. By forcibly stopping such behaviours and not replacing them with something positive, or a sense of calmness - we can put our pet's mental well-being under further stress. By removing undesirable behavior, we are not removing the underlying cause for it. Due to this, it maybe that over time, the animal could start to display another behaviour to replace it. Due to the fact that their original problem is still there and the associated feelings are continuing to be experienced.

By getting to the cause of why the animal feels the need to display such behavior, we can help them address their emotional, environmental and pain related issues to help aid them in disposing of a behaviour that is no longer serving them.

When problems are not addressed, or are addressed but in the wrong way, behaviours are open to becoming worse - sometimes even dangerous. By stifling such a problem, we are in danger of creating another problem, or even causing the animal partial or even full mental breakdown.

The behaviour can escalate to the point that the animal is a real danger to itself and others and completely beyond safe control.

They may retreat into their own world as a way of avoiding total mental collapse, even display mental illnesses - such as self-induced Autism or trance states. In either case the animal will become ungrounded and have little awareness of 'self'. It will reside in its own world. Some animals will give the appearance of going through all the correct physical steps whilst not being completely 'present'. They may stop showing any form of emotion and their negative display of behaviour in certain cases may stop. Unfortunately, when these behaviours stop, and the animal appears quieter and more at rest. It can give the less experienced observer the view that the animal is feeling better when in actual fact, the animal has mentally and emotionally shut down to the point of being almost robotic like - due to the lack of being able to 'feel'.

Multiple Personality Syndrome

This can be recognised in animals by deciphering some kinds of sudden behaviour changes. Also referred to as a 'Jackal and Hyde' type personality.

It would appear that Multiple Personality Syndrome in animals could fall into two categories.

Dis-Integration

Meaning that the animal's personality has become fragmented. Usually attributed to emotional trauma or faulty chemical systems within the physical body. In human cases of MPS, it has been found that fluctuations in bio-chemicals and neuropeptides can lead to such disorders. There appears to be no logical reason why such fluctuations in these chemicals should not cause the same types of mental illness in animals. However, there is very little if any research carried out on this subject. In the case of severe emotional trauma, it is possible for an animal to invent one or more new personas. These personalities not only appear to have a mind of their own, but usually will also have a whole past history of that 'individual's' life.

It has been noted in the case of human MPS that not only does the person take on a new identity whilst the secondary (or third as the case maybe) personality is dominant, but the physical body may also take on that personalities illnesses or allergies. It should be noted however, that these illnesses and allergies are only present when the related personality is in place. They can disappear as quickly as they came.

This can cause problems sometimes - for example: If one personality is allergic to a certain food substance it can be avoided whilst the associated personality is present. However, if the food allergen is still in digestive transit within the body when the allergy prone personality is present, this can then lead to an allergic reaction.

Outside Influence

Experiments carried out have already shown us that the mind or 'psyche', as it is sometimes referred to, is separate and not directly connected to the brain or the physical body. It has been shown that the mind is able to enter or leave the physical body by choice. This is often the case in animals presenting mental illnesses such as self-induced Autism and trance like states. Though an animal exhibiting these types of mental illness will not automatically also suffer from MPS.

It is not uncommon for another consciousness to make its home in the animal's physical body. In such cases it is often possible to have the 'bogus' personality removed from the animal. This should be carried out by someone who is suitably experienced in these types of cases. When this is carried out correctly - the unwanted behaviour will slowly diminish. It should be noted that it could take time, as the behaviour may have become habitual if the problem has been going on for a while.

Recognising MPS through Communication

As our communication with an animal works through our intention to connect with their mind. We can choose to communicate with whatever consciousness or part of the animal's consciousness is choosing to exhibit the behaviour.

In the same why as we intend to connect with a certain animal, we can intend to connect to the consciousness responsible for the behaviour. When we do this, we may find that we feel like we are communicating with a totally different personality altogether. The voice that we hear may soften or come across as harsh and stronger, and may even change gender in style.

Once we have connected to this personality, we can ask them who they are and what their intentions are. This can give us insight as to what is going on, if the primary animal personality is unable to clarify the situation or is unaware of it.

It has been claimed in human cases of MPS that the primary personality has no knowledge of the secondary personality. However, in cases of animal MPS there are some animals that are indeed aware of their other personalities. Though it tends to be more in cases of external personalities rather than fragmentation of the primary.

The Animal's Environment

The animal's environment plays a huge role in their physical and emotional well-being. This can encompass all manner of things from basic physical needs such as food, to mental stimulation and love. When something is not right within the environment where the animals spends most of its time, it can lead to physical and emotional issues.

Environmental Needs

Company (With the same species as well as others and the owner)

Diet (Suited to the animal's species and the individual)

Suitable bed and shelter

Regular exercise (Depending on species)

Appropriate veterinary care

Discipline and training

Clean living environment

An understanding of where they fit within the 'family' or pecking order

Love and physical contact

The Owners Influence

As many of our animals spend a lot of their time in our company rather than with their own species, it is not at all unusual for them to become humanised.

This can come in several forms including:

Diet

Eating human foods rather than foods best suited to their species.

Behaviour

Taking on the role of the 'parents' child.

When we have pets it is very easy to come to love them in a maternal way. This of course is good from the point of view that we care for them and love them. But we must remember that they have their own needs, be they species related, or simply the need to be acknowledged as an individual.

When we treat an animal as a fellow human. We take away much of their natural nature and instinct, often making them live in houses, not having much contact with others of their own species and encouraging or even making them - fit into our own way of living.

By feeding animals our own foods or specially made pet processed foods, we can take away their natural hunting instincts and dietary requirements. Many pet owners who love their animals as if they were their children choose to spoil them. This may include letting them get away with behaviour that is seen as unsuitable by others (often caused by distress at the situation they find themselves in), whilst making excuses as to why these behaviours are acceptable.

Observations by animal rescue staff have found that animals that are spoilt can be harder to rehabilitate than animals that have been abused. Whilst finding that the hardest animals to rehabilitate are animals that have been neglected. By neglected, I am referring to animals that have minimal interaction with others - both human and animal - rather than a lack of good food and medical care.

In the wild, most species that we choose to keep as pets would choose to live in herds, flocks or packs. Within these set orders they would have a pecking order, meaning that each individual knows their place within the group they find themselves. Part of helping to keep our pets mentally balanced, is to help them to understand where exactly they fit within the home and human family. The secret of this of course is consistency in training methods and instruction, as well as welcoming them into our home as a valuable individual member in the correct way.

WHAT ARE WE REALLY TELLING THEM?

Animals are very open to reading the thoughts of not only other animals, but also those of their owners and other people that come into their environment. What we think or say consciously, does not always gel correctly with our subconscious understanding, needs or desires. Whilst we may think we are saying or believing one thing, it may well be that deep down we know different, or believe in something else entirely and this is where the confusion can lie. No matter how much we convince our self of something, our animals will always see our true intentions and thoughts. It may be that we believe we are thinking in a certain way and backing that up with the relevant body language. However, it may be that at the same time we are not fully resonating with our true belief and understanding of the situation. By the mere fact that we are sending out conflicting information subconsciously (and therefore truthfully on that level) we can often misinform our animals as to what we really mean.

This can lead to two different reactions from the animal. Either the animal will react to our true thoughts and act accordingly, which can lead us to believe that they are not understanding us correctly or are going against our wishes. Or, the animal can become confused by the conflicting information and become disorientated due to not knowing quite what we are asking them to do. By being as honest with ourselves as we can possibly be, and learning to accept and recognise our fears when they are present, we can give our animals much clearer information as to what is really going on.

Example

A lady has a pet cat that shares her home with her. She works long hours and often asks someone else to come in and feed her cat for her. As much as she needs the person to enter her home and feed her cat, she is not happy at having someone in her home whilst she isn't there.

The cat then attacks the person who comes to feed him, believing that he is guarding her home as she is telling him that she doesn't want people entering her house when she isn't there. At the same time, the lady honestly believes that she is telling her cat not to attack the person who comes to feed him, as she needs the person to do it.

Such a scenario - when viewed from the outside - could lead us to believe that the cat is showing all the signs of a behaviour problem. In truth, the cat is just carrying out the subconscious requests of his owner by trying to protect her home. As he is fully aware of her not wanting people in her home whilst she is at work.

Situations such as these are very common, especially when an element of fear from the animal's owner is being suppressed, to the point that they are not even fully aware of it themselves. In these kinds of situations, rather than reprimanding the animal for their behavior, we have to look at our own thoughts and fears and change them accordingly to enable us to instruct our pets in a way that gives the desired and most favorable outcome all round.

The Animal as a Healer

Just as many of us have a natural ability to heal and help others, so do animals. It is commonly known of the wonderful results that swimming with dolphins can bring. In more recent years horses have also played a vital role in human healing due to their intuitive and loving nature, as well as them being more readily accessible to the general public.

Within all relationships experienced in our lifetime, there are lessons to be learnt and experiences to be had. So long as we choose to view the positive in all of our experiences, no experience can be seen as truly bad or wasted.

Many animals come into people's lives as Healers and to teach them of self-worth, understanding and even death. It maybe that you set out to find a particular breed or species of animal, only to find yourself drawn to something completely different. If this happens, go with your gut instinct - as chances are the animal you are being drawn to is one that you need to learn from, or experience with. In such cases our 'chosen' animal may come to us in unusual or obscure ways, such as a kitten left in a box on our doorstep, or a dog we are asked to give a home to, even though we had no intention of having another dog.

Studies have shown the benefits of keeping animals and the happiness they can bring. This can range from children with learning disabilities who progress against the odds once a new pet has come into the family - to people with high blood pressure who gradually manage to maintain an even pressure when in the presence of a much loved pet. This is largely down to the relaxation that takes place due to the release of the chemical Oxytocin.

This is the same chemical hormone that both animal

and human females experience during pregnancy and after birth. It is often referred to as the 'cuddle hormone'.

The Second Heart Chakra

Whilst working with my horses in 1995, I was shown a chakra that is light green in colour and is present in the flank of many species of animals. Although linked to the animals' energy systems, it is not directly part of these systems. The animals use this chakra whilst giving healing to others as a way of taking on the negative energies of others and transmuting them. For many animals the taking on of this role is very emotional and brings with it much responsibility. For this reason, the second heart chakra may remain closed in some animals until such a time comes that they feel comfortable enough both emotionally and physically to take on their role as a Healer.

Under no circumstances should the second heart chakra be opened in any animal that is not yet really. To open this chakra prematurely could bring the animal emotional distress.

ETHICS AND LEGALITIES

With regards to treating an animal in person the law states:

Protection of Animals Act 1911

Legally the owner of any animal may give appropriate treatment so long as it is not considered physically invasive.

The veterinary surgery (exemptions) order of 1962

It is illegal for any complementary therapy to be administered to an animal by anyone other than the animal's owner, unless veterinary permission is first granted.

Please Note:

Healing is not a replacement for veterinary care and attention. Anyone who allows an animal to suffer through withholding veterinary attention can be prosecuted.

It is illegal for anyone other than a veterinary surgeon to diagnose an animal. However, you may pass on any information that the animal is giving that can then be passed onto the animal's Veterinary Surgeon. This may go a long way in helping their Vet with a medical diagnosis. Even if you find yourself in the situation where the animal is telling you directly that it has a certain illness. It is best advised that the information given by the animal is passed on - rather than the actual diagnosis. That is best left to the medical profession.

Whilst animal communication by some peoples understanding falls into the realm of psychic, it is without a doubt a very important role we play with regards to an animal's physical and emotional welfare. In order to be taken seriously we must remember to work from a professional point of view at all times, knowing our limits and boundaries and working within them.

It is my personal view that the word 'psychic' should for this reason not be linked to animal communication. It can give the wrong impression and even discredit the wonderful work many communicators are doing.

It maybe that you are in a veterinary waiting room and a dog that is waiting to be seen starts to tell you all about their illness. At this point we must remember that the owner has chosen to bring their dog to the vet and not us. If you feel you can help, you may feel comfortable engaging in conversation with the owner and asking what is wrong with their animal.

At this stage there is no need to explain to them what you do, or what you are hearing. It might just be that if the owner is happy to chat to you and that you are able to make helpful suggestions. If however you gain little response to your suggestion or questioning, it may be best left well alone. It must be remembered that not everyone is open to animal communication and those who are aware of it, or even those who have not yet encountered it, may fear it. If this is the case by charging in and giving your two pence worth, you might upset or even alienate the animal's owner. This of course is also not professional from the point of view that at this time you are sat in a veterinary waiting room with someone else's client.

In other more relaxed situations, you might feel comfortable to explain to people what you do and that you feel you could help their animal. It is one thing to comment, 'What a happy dog you have' and quite another to comment to say, 'Your dog is telling me your husband bullies you'. If the owner has stated that they are happy for you to communicate with their animal and would like to hear what they have to say, then all well and good. But it is inadvisable to push yourself forwards in a way that may upset people.

The Permission Issue

People tend to have different views about this issue. With regards to healing, permission is very important and should only be given with the intention of it being for the animal's highest good. The reason being, that by healing a certain emotional problem or physical issue that they have, we may well be taking away their ability to deal with it or heal it themselves. Which in some cases, is needed for their own learning and understanding.

On the communication front do we need the animal's permission? Logic would say that if an animal doesn't want to talk to us, then we can't make them, so many would see this as a clearly given answer.

However, where do we stand on communicating with someone else's pet when they haven't given their permission, or have openly asked us not to? In these circumstances it very much comes down to how you feel about it and what you are willing or not willing to do. Firstly, we can question whether we need the owner's permission at all. As surely we do not need permission to speak with another living being from someone else, if the animal obviously wants to talk. Surely this decision should be left entirely up to the animal?

An owner's refusal to allow you to communicate with their pet might be through fear of animal communication its self, or stem from a concern that their beloved pet might give away their darkest secrets. Whether or not you choose to communicate with an animal under these circumstances is very much a personal choice, but the free will of the animal should always be taken into consideration. It might just be that by communicating with the animal you will be helping them a great deal emotionally.

When People Don't Like What They Hear

There is always the possibility that an animal's owner isn't comfortable with what it is that you are telling them. If what you are giving the animal's owner is an answer stemming from a question they have asked you to query their pet about, then logic would say that they should be open to hearing that answer. However, answers aren't always happily accepted. In these cases you have done your job correctly and carried out what you have been asked to do. If the client has an issue with the answer then this is in no way down to you and it is for them to work through.

If an animal volunteers information of a personal nature about the owner or the owners family. Then it is advisable to ask the client first if they are open to hearing it. This way you are not leaving yourself open to over stepping the mark and causing upset.

The Sceptic's Challenge

You will always come across people who are sceptical of things such as animal communication. They want to catch you out and test you at every opportunity. Ultimately there is only one person who you have to convince of your ability, and that is you. Over time, you will come across people who say, 'If you can't tell me who my dog's best friend is then you can't do it'. Ride over such comments and let them go. To try and convince a true sceptic is a very hard thing to do. With most of them no amount of accurate information will convince them. With many of them the bottom line is that they don't want to believe in the existence of animal communication, so never will. Your job isn't to convince people of its existence. Your job is to help the animals that are brought to you.

When faced with a sceptic's challenge just politely tell them that you are busy and maybe recommend some books on animal communication that they might like to read. In giving you this challenge they are simply wanting to see your downfall so they can say 'I told you so'. When we are put in such situations, our stress levels rise and straight away we make things much harder for ourselves. For these reasons it would be advisable to steer clear of such situations, as there is no reason at all for you to be challenged by anyone over the existence of animal communication. If they truly wish to find out about it, there is plenty of information available.

THE ANIMALS' PRAYER

Pray with me for now I am blessed
You lay your hands upon my chest
As my heart beats hard and strong
Hear my words, my sacred song
Let me heal you too my friend
Let our loving connection know no end

As our hearts they beat as one
Come with me for we are now as one
As I guide you through your life
I share with you your joys and strife
I am your trusted friend you see
By your side, you destiny

Our paths have crossed through eons of time
Take my blessing as a sign

This wondrous path, the one we tread
You lay your hands upon my head
I'll show you what you need to see
The purpose, the truth, the reality

Be at one with who you are
Take my hand I'll lead you far
In the darkness of the night
I will be your shining light
I raise you up from all despair
With me the love is always there

May your life be filled with joy and grace
As I place my paws upon your face
This healing calm within your soul
Together we can reach our goal
So now my friend the time is near
For you to let go of your fear

I'm here to catch you when you fall
With graceful wings we upward soar
As you true life purpose comes into view
I will be here gently holding you
As you softly call my name
Your life will never be the same
As you walk upon with me
You know our love can set us free

TRACKING LOST AND STOLEN ANIMALS

It is a sad fact that every year in the UK, thousands of family pets are either lost or stolen. Tracking a lost or stolen animal can put a Communicator under a huge amount of pressure for several reasons:

The animal maybe constantly on the move.

If the animal is very distressed, it may have trouble communicating.

You may pick up on the residual energy of where they have been rather than where they are.

If you work with Animal Guides, you may want to ask them for any input or insights that they may have. Start by communicating with the animal in the way that you normally would.

Suggested Questions

Do they feel safe?

Are they injured?

Are they hungry?

What do they see around them?

Do they know where they are?

Have they been taken in by someone?

Did they leave of their own accord, or were they taken?

Do they know why it happened?

Can they see anything that they can mentally show you as a clue to where they are?

As well as asking questions, we can also work with something known as 'remote viewing'. This involves astrally projecting (our consciousness leaving the body) and going to where the animal is. This can be done during meditation. We can then imagine being in the air above the animal and viewing them and their surrounds. By doing this we may see landmarks, or even signposts with names on.

Alternatively we can ask an animal to show us what

it is seeing through its eyes. When this happens you may find yourself watching what looks like a film.

Tracking missing animals is always hard and can be very hit and miss. Don't be disheartened if you are unable to help to locate an animal, as it may be the next one you are asked to work with is found safe and sound.

The Energetic Dynamics Behind The Disappearance

As with everything, an energetic blueprint is made in order that the physical reality can then manifest. Through meditation we can imagine the missing animal behind a closed door, the other side of the door being the animal's way home. We can then step through the door to see what is the other side of it and is stopping the animal from entering through the door and returning home. By removing such obstacles we can help to alter the energetic dynamic and hopefully help the animal either to find their way home, or to be found.

The Animal's Life Path

All animals have a destined path to walk in much the same way as we do. Life is free will for animals, but they often feel obliged to live the way we want them to. Due to them often finding themselves in unfavorable circumstances, they are sometimes unable to complete what they came here to do. We have already previously discussed how 'chosen' animals may come to us under strange circumstances. When we don't listen to our intuition and follow what we need to do, not only are we affecting our own destiny, but also that of the animal involved.

Karma

Karma is created when we wrong someone, or they do something to us that they shouldn't. When this happens we create what is known as a 'Karmic debt' towards that person or animal. Sooner or later that debt will need to be paid back. It maybe that the animal or person who we need to work the debt through with, comes into contact with us in this life time - or the debt may be carried over to the next life time. Until the debt is paid, the cycle will be on going. This is where the phrases, 'What goes around comes around' and 'You reap what you sow', come from.

It maybe that within the relationship with your animals, all karmic debts have been cleared in past lifetimes, or that there were never any such debts to be paid. It could be that your animal found their way to you, as you were the right person to put them in the position to enable them to complete their life lesson or task this time around.

Examples

To enable them to fulfill their role as a Healer.

To help them pass on important information to help either yourself or others.

So that they can be close to another person or animal to work through a karmic debt.

You might be an intermediate stop for them finding the person they are meant to be with.

To enable them to become physically or emotionally well so they may continue their work.

Whatever the reason for your pet finding their way to you, in time you will come to understand it and help them progress spiritually and fulfill their life's quest.

As with all living things there will come a time when the animal is ready to leave the physical plane. Obviously the more pain free and quieter this is for them the better. Animals view death a little differently from most people, in as much as they see it as just another part of the ongoing cycle of life. Though of course, that is not to say that some aren't desperate to stay with their friends and family in many cases. They have an acceptance of death to a large degree and don't fear it as we do. When we come to accept this, we make it far easier for our much-loved family pets to leave us when their time has come. When an animal is elderly and is in pain, or when our pet has been unwell for a long time with no chance of recovery, why mourn their death when we can rejoice in their life and the memories we shared?

Who are we crying for - the animal who has returned 'home', or for our self?

To love an animal one hundred percent is to let them go when their time has come. To hold them close and tell them that it's all right for them to go. That we love them and wish them well. To then close our eyes and imagine the energetic cords that connect us to them. Visualise yourself cutting the cords with love, whilst watching them slowly float away. This is the action of true love. Think of the good times and the lessons learnt and you will see that their life was never wasted. Death can be beautiful when we can see the bigger picture and interpret it as such.

It may even be that you find yourself taking in all kinds of animals that despite your best efforts, you are unable to make well. Maybe you just happen to be the right person they can feel safe with so that they feel they can go. Maybe that is your part to play in their healing - their release.

All too often the people I meet feel guilty about their animal's illness or passing. They feel that they didn't do enough to help them in their hour of need. When I meet people who have these thoughts I ask them - 'Did you do everything you were mentally and physically capable of doing?' More often than not the answer is 'yes'. I then gently explain to them that this being the case, they have done nothing wrong. Sometimes to hear this from another person is enough to reverse years of guilt, though of course nothing can be as wonderful as hearing this information from their pet themselves.

True love doesn't blame, hold resentment or ever die.
It is eternal.

Past-Life Memories and Injures

It is not at all unusual for animals to talk about other life times they have experienced, even lives as a human. Some people still view animals as their underlings and have a hard time acknowledging that animals have had lives as humans. As your communication skills progress and your mind expands and accepts new possibilities, this understanding will become perfectly acceptable to you.

Past-life information may come in several ways:

The animal may show you images of themselves in another

body.

The animal may talk about 'when I was....'

They might say to you 'When I was with you before....'

Or you may just have a feeling of 'knowing' an animal during your first encounter with them.

The memories that we hold within our electromagnetic energy field are carried with us from lifetime to lifetime. Within the field our past memories, experiences and energetic disruptions also exist. They accompany us to our present lifetime. When we suffer illnesses or injures in past lives, we weaken part of the aura. This can make an animal susceptible to new illnesses manifesting. The emotional traumas experienced in these other life times our held within the subconscious. These can sometimes lead to psychosomatic allergies, phobias and seemingly irrational fears. By working through these fears and traumas and finding out how and why they began - we can start to heal them. Part of the way we can work towards this is by helping the animal to remain in the here and now - enabling them to understand what was 'then' and what is 'now'. Working energetically with the aura will also help in the mending process.

Giving Thanks

It should be remembered at all times that animals don't have to speak to us. Nor do they need to help us - they choose to. At all times this should be appreciated and understood. Always 'thank' an animal for their help and for speaking with you, as often a 'thank you' goes a long way. Asking them if there is anything you can do for them is always a nice way to repay the favor.

CHOOSE YOUR TITLE CAREFULLY

What is actually in a title?

What is the purpose?

Why is it so important?

Our title tells people who we are and what we do. When we do not give ourselves a correct title it can cause people to misunderstand what we do and what we are about. I tend to use the title 'Animal Communicator', as this is what I do and who I am. It is my role and vocation in life and an innate part of who I am. Quite simply put: my career is one of communicating with animals and helping them to be heard, as well as helping their human Guardians too.

Sadly there are labels that are being used that are not necessarily in the best interests of our work and for explaining what it is that we do. These are titles such as Pet Psychic and Animal Psychic – Pet Medium and Animal Medium. I must admit that these titles make me cringe. The reason being, that they can bring about the dial a psychic for £1.50 a minute, ideas to mind. The 'spooky ' your cat has a white spot on his chest' communicators, whose client exclaim they are 'correct' and 'wow'. Is this really what we are and how we want to be viewed? Further more is this actually productive for animals? Let's face it, the cat with a white spot on his chest knows he has a white spot as does his Guardian. So what actually is gained in such a communication and the passing on of this information? The information that needs to be passed on is far more important than that. Imagine living in a foreign country and only being able to speak the native language for an hour of your life. There is far more important information that needs to be heard and passed on in order to help in the creation of change for the better for that animal.

Further to this, using words such as 'psychic' can also stop us, and the information offered from the animal, from being taken seriously by some individuals. A classically trained Vet is more likely to be open minded and interested to as what the role of an 'Animal Communicator' is and what they do, than he is of an Animal Psychic that he may choose to instantly dismiss as 'hocus pocus' due to title alone.

Whilst it is fair to say that many Animal Communicators are psychic and that many also work as Mediums. Titling yourself as such, or mixing your animal work with Mediumship, can be misleading and bring about the wrong impression. It may even cause a loss of credibility. Not just for yourself, but also for other Animal Communicators. I have no doubt that some Communicators will be feeling that in saying this I am being a little judgmental.

But rather than looking at it that way, consider instead how others may view it.

Including those clients who have pets that are sick, have behaviour problems and are in need of your help. As the reason that I am choosing to explain this, even knowing it may cause offence for some, is to try and help the animal communication movement as a whole. To help aid us in getting the recognition that we rightfully deserve.

For this reason my advice would be to label your self wisely. Instead of taking offence at what I have said, look at the bigger picture. Look at how other people may view you and the kind of clients it may cause you to attract. As well as how it may cause you and others to be viewed.

Animal communication is a form of Mediumship, but that does not mean it needs to be associated with 'talking to dead people' and 'I have your grandmother Florence here with the pink hair'.

Your title alone will have a huge affect on how people view not only you, but also others on this chosen path.

I have also come across some Communicators that have chosen to give themselves strange names, rather than using their everyday names. Again this brings to mind the word 'psychic' and can cause people to put you into the 'mystical' category. This is not what we need to be aiming for and though whilst some may find it draws to them the kind of clients they like, it may not be the case that through the type of 'readings' that they are doing, that they are working to the best of their ability. In instances such as these it will only be the animals that suffer.

Animal Communication is a serious subject and it needs to be treated as such.

Recently I put an animal communication consultation up as a prize in a raffle to help raise money for horse sanctuary. I was given the name of the person that had won it by the organiser and I emailed her. I asked her for the age, name and gender of her horse. Along with any white face markings and what she would like me to ask her horse about for her. Her reply came back that I would be glad to hear that her mother was one of the best known psychics in England. She said that she thought that I would be pleased as that meant she believed in this kind of psychic connection.

My heart sank - just these three lines alone showed what she thought my role was and that she thought me a psychic that 'reads' horses for entertainment. Her comment that it was good news to me as it meant she believed in this kind of psychic connection just went to further show me that she was a 'tester' and was not fully understanding my work - its importance and my role in helping them both.

She also asked me, could she not divulge any information and that I just 'read' her horse to see what I got. I politely messaged her back explaining that I am not a psychic and my connection is a direct connection with the horse. My reasoning for asking for questions is that all animals are different. Some are chatty and have open personalities - whilst some are not so, so it is always good to have some questions handy, as a way of starting off conversation and that it also enables the Guardian to find out about what they need to - based on their concerns. Not only this, but this is the way that I have been working in my profession all of these years. That I consider myself an Animal

Communicator and Therapist and not a Psychic that does readings for entertainment.

I was told then that the 'prize' should be re-raffled as it was no use to her, as there was nothing wrong with her horse. That reply I felt was a bit of a shame. This lady did not know whether or not her horse may have a virus that showed no external symptoms that may have been sat there for years knocking the immune system. She did not know if her horse was lame, as it may have been experiencing a masked pain, so that he did not present as lame visually.

Her total dismissing of the communication was because she expected me to be a psychic reader, whose job was telling people things about their horses that they already knew. What is the point in that? To take and use it as some sort of entertainment, dependent on whether it fit in with what she thought about her horse or not. This is not and will never be the kind of person I wish to work for.

What is the point?

When someone is this closed minded as to think there is nothing wrong with their horse? In all my years of animal communication which has clocked up literally thousands of communications with horses. The least number if physical issues I have ever found in any one horse is three. This was a three year old horse that belonged to an Equine

Physiotherapist. This lady had not even stopped to consider that her horse had feelings, may need his voice heard and had issues that she was unaware of.

It is totally understandable that there are sceptics out there. I personally feel that until someone fully experiences or learns about it, then a degree of open minded scepticism is healthy. I have come across too many clients that are all too willing to pay any amount and believe anything they are told - that concerns me. There have even been times that I have pulled clients to one side and gently explained to them, that there are charlatans and not everyone loves animals and wants to help in the way they profess they want to.

Another common title used by Animal Communicators is 'Horse Whisper', or 'Animal Whisper'. Again these titles can be misleading. 'Whispering' refers to the observation and assessment of an animal's body language. It is not the same connection that we use in animal communication. 'Whispers' tend to work more with training animals and engaging with them by reading the subtle cues that they are displaying physically. This should not be confused with the telepathic connection that Animal Communicators have with animals. That said, many Animal Communicators also choose to work with Whispering in addition to their animal communication work. These two ways of communicating with animals work well together, even though there are obvious difference between the two types of approach and the dynamics involved.

ARE ANIMALS PYSCHIC OR INTUITIVE?

Which would you consider yourself to be?

Do you 'read' the animal, or do you have a direct line of communication with them?

Do you consider yourself 'psychic' and what does psychic even mean?

'"Relating to or denoting faculties or phenomena that are apparently inexplicable by natural laws".

"Psychic powers"

Words associated with psychic:

Supernatural, paranormal, other-worldly, supernormal, preternatural, metaphysical, extrasensory, transcendental, magic, magical, mystical, mystic and occult.

There is nothing paranormal about animal communication anymore than there is anything mystical about it. Animal communication is simply a natural sense and ability that we all have and that is innate to us. It simply enables us to mentally travel and connect to and with, an animal on a subtle level. Enabling us to decipher the subtle information and knowledge that exists within them and that they are aware of.

Yes, the experience may feel mystical, transcendental and magical, but this is all just part of how we relate to it and how it feels to us. The connection of two energies is simple physics and natural. It is an innate ability that we all have and to a large degree as humans, deny not only to ourselves, but by consequence to the animal kingdom as well.

Now let us look at the word "Intuitive".

Intuitive meaning - based on what one feels to be true even without conscious reasoning; instinctive.

Words associated with the word "intuitive".

Instinctive, intuitional and instinctual.

Now do those meanings in reference to animal communication sit more comfortably to you?

When we communicate with an animal it is not just about what we hear - but also what we feel. This may come as a gut instinct, or just a 'knowing' that what we are hearing is correct, or just does not feel right. This then may cause us to start to question down another line of enquiry that will bring about an outcome that has aided the animal and their Guardian.

It is not just about what we hear, it is also about gathering together and working out, all of the additional information that comes with it.

Psychic and intuitive are very different and one should not become confused with the other. Whilst it is fair to say that most Communicators will work with both psychic ability and intuition. I feel it is safe to say that the most forth coming and important communications will come through our intuitive abilities and our rational ones.

'Reading' an animal is very different to 'direct connection' with them. The reading of an animal is a third party opinion of that animal, if the information is being 'given' and 'offered' to you by another source. If you are reading the animal yourself, there is no problem with this at all, so long as you are reading them correctly. I just feel that it is important to understand the difference between reading and direct communication. As strictly speaking the reading of an animal is not really animal communication.

The direct communication with an animal enables us to ask questions and hear information from them first hand. What we should also be aware of too, is that what we choose to hear is the animal's own version of the story - as they saw and experienced it. What one individual may see and experience in one way - may be very different from the next animal's personal experience, or even how the Guardian has experienced and felt about it. For this reason it is always important to bare in mind that the opinion of an animal may be biased when they are choosing to speak out for all of their species. They may be that they are only be speaking on behalf of certain individuals within that species as well as themselves without being aware of that fact. Some may have different feelings about an event, experience, their species or situation entirely.

So are animals psychic?

Yes and no - it depends very much on how an animal (the same as a person) directs their energy towards others and deciphers another's energy. A dog that can sniff out cancer or detect the early onset of a seizure is not psychic. He is simply picking up on the electromagnetic changes of the body's energy, the change in brain wave pattern (if this should be the case) and the change in the chemicals in the person or animal's body through his olfactory system. There is nothing remotely psychic about that and it is just all part of the innate sense that an animal uses, that to a large degree has been lost by humans.

Some Communicators will tell stories of animals that have foretold the future and been correct. So should be consider this psychic? Well indeed it may fall into those realms and the description of its meaning.

Let us not forget what an animal truly is. They are a soul, a consciousness with a physical body that enables them (like us) to live out an earthy experience and evolve and hopefully progress. If the assumption holds true that we journey through many life times, then it would also stand to reason that those events, experiences and memories of other life times, would be held still within that consciousness. This taken into consideration then no - it is not of any wonder that animals can speak the way they do about having lived through other life times, as well as their relaying of information that you would not have expected them to be able to other wise gain.

There are many things that science has yet to understand and prove. Science will only ever be as good and keeping up with the times, as those that are within the scientific field.

A good book for understanding more about the mental link that some animals have with their Guardians is:

'Dogs that know when their owner's are coming home' - *Rupert Sheldrake.*

WHY ASK FOR QUESTIONS

Like people, animals all have their own unique personalities. Some are more 'chatty' and forth coming than others, whilst some choose to hold back when in the presence of new company, or any company other than a few close friends. Due to this, it is always wise to have some questions handy from the animal's Guardian.

This will also enable you to know how best to direct the communication from the point of view of what information is being looked for. If for instance an animal is in pain and that pain is long standing. They may not choose to mention it as it has become part of everyday life for them. They may have developed a high pain threshold and just 'deal with it' and accept it on a daily basis. The animal may also be aware that the Guardian knows about the pain. Due to this, in an open communication where questions are not asked the animal may not even mention it.

This is one of the many reasons why questions are so important. It also may be that an issue or problem that the animal has, they may feel is not able to be sorted. Again, due to this it may be something that they then choose not to bother voicing unless asked.

Without asking the relevant questions, we may end up just throwing up random pieces of information that in the long run is of no use to the animal and their Guardian. By working on a question and answer type basis, it will not only help with animals that feel they have little to say, but means that that what is needed to be voiced and brought to light can be.

Another example of this is in cases where an animal has a degenerative issue with their sight or hearing. The degeneration may have been slow so that they may not have really noticed it much. Due to this, they may not choose to voice that they have an issue with one or either, as they are not actually aware of it themselves. Through asking them about it, it causes them to focus on it in a way that may bring it to light. Another way that we can also access issues such as these. Is to ask the animal to allow us to see through their eyes and hear through their ears as they do. By doing this we can see and hear if there is any difference between the two ears or eyes and any loss or distortion.

ASSESSING PAIN LEVELS

This is a subject that a lot of Animal Communicators tell me that they struggle with. Just how do you assess pain levels in someone else, or an animal other than by physical observation and heart rate?

I have found that the easily way to go about this is to use a score chart. I use zero to mean no pain is being experienced in that area and ten to mean unbearable pain. I then ask the animal to give me a figure based on over all average pain and another figure for when the pain is at its worst.

Bare in mind too - issues such as arthritis may change in their pain levels, dependent on the time of year. They may get worse during seasons that have a lot of cold and damp weather. Intermittent and sharp, sudden pains also may score differently at different times.

We also need to take into consideration the difference between observation of physically presenting symptoms and each individual's pain threshold. If an animal has long term pain that they have had to live with. Chances are they are used to it to a degree and that the symptoms may not present themselves visually, in the same way that they would do in cases of acute pain. Whilst one animal may still be walking on a lame leg, another animal with equally as much pain may choose not to weight bare at all.

Some animals will have been prescribed pain relief by their Veterinary Surgeon. This may be for acute or chronic issues. In the case of chronic issues I always advise my client's to also look into additional and alternative types of pain relief. This may come in the form of aromatics, homeopathy or therapies that will further help with pain management rather, than just going down the drug route alone.

Animals can suffer unbearable pain and yet at the same time not really physically present it. There are several symptoms that should be looked out for and are also a good indicator as to their levels being experienced.

Head pressing against walls or other flat objects

Head banging

Unusually immobile and choosing not to move around much

Abnormal or very obviously extended sleeping patterns

A change in behaviour such as having little tolerance and becoming easily frustrated

Violent behaviour or outbursts that are out of character for the individual

Refusing to eat their everyday food or taking an abnormal lack of interest in it

If an animal is in pain, it is important to stress to the animal's Guardian that action needs to be taken in the form of some kind of medical intervention to try and stop further suffering immediately. There are also many other avenues that then can be additionally explored to aid the animal further.

If a clients pet is in pain they need to see a qualified Veterinary Surgeon for assessment and treatment.

THE FINE LINE OF DIAGNOSING

So what is diagnosing and where is the line drawn?

If we see a cat hopping on three legs and holding up its forth leg due to pain and we say 'that cat is lame'? - are we then diagnosing? If so, then most people that work with, or have animals in their daily lives, are breaking the law on a regular basis - according to the Veterinary Surgeons Act 19.2 (a).

When it comes to diagnosis the Veterinary Surgeons Act 1996 states:

19.1 The purpose of this guidance is to explain the restrictions that apply under the Veterinary Surgeons Act 1966 ('the Act') to ensure that animals are treated only by those people qualified to do so. These restrictions apply where the 'treatment' is considered to be the practice of 'veterinary surgery', as defined by the Act.

19.2 Section 19 of the Act provides, subject to a number of exceptions, that only registered members of the Royal College of Veterinary Surgeons may practise veterinary surgery. 'Veterinary surgery' is defined within the Act as follows:

'Veterinary Surgery means the art and science of veterinary surgery and medicine and, without prejudice to the generality of the foregoing, shall be taken to include -

a. the diagnosis of diseases in, and injuries to, animals including tests performed on animals for diagnostic purposes;

b. the giving of advice based upon such diagnosis;

c. the medical or surgical treatment of animals; and

d. the performance of surgical operations on animals.'

The Veterinary Surgeons Act is a double edged sword. Whilst it aims to protect animals from charlatans and safe guard their physical welfare. It also limits the ability of certain qualified individuals that are excellent in their chosen field and career, in their ability to help animals in need. This can be seen all too easily by the handful of Veterinary Surgeons that choose to not give their permission for other professionals such as Osteopaths and Chiropractors to assess and treat some animals. Even in the absence of them themselves, being able to provide a valid diagnosis and treatment.

So where do Animal Communicators stand?

There is a fine line in regards to diagnosing as already discussed. When we pass on information from an animal are we actually diagnosing? If an animal is telling us about their symptoms and we are relaying that information to the animal's Guardian, or their Veterinary Surgeon, how exactly are we diagnosing? We are not looking at the animal physically and making a clinical diagnosis based on our own findings. In the case of body scanning we are passing in information relating to energetic disruptions found - not physical ones. Maybe aided by the information also given to us by the animal in question that is having the actual experience.

Whether or not the Veterinary Surgeon or Guardian choose to take this information up, is beyond our control. But for the animal's sake if this information has been offered by them, the one that is in fact experiencing those symptoms - surely it in within our duty to pass that information on?

Any medical issues that do come to light, should be voiced to the animal's Guardian with the advice that they seek medical advice from their Vet for it. They can also choose to research alternatives and things that are additional and may help. First point of call should be, and needs to be their Veterinary Surgeon. They are suitably qualified and have the knowledge needed, and apparatus available, to make a proper and informed clinical diagnosis which is much needed.

Animal communication in cases of health issues, is in addition to correct care from the animal's Veterinary Surgeon. It is not, and should not, be considered a replacement for it.

That said, every week I come across clients that have animals, for which their Veterinary Surgeons have not been able to give a firm medical diagnosis. Without such a diagnosis it makes it hard to give a prognosis and a course of correct treatment. On going lameness issues and general lethargy are often the cases that I come across. It is not unusual for animals to have a lingering virus that continually knocks their immune system. Whilst providing no external symptoms other than fatigue. In some species this can easily be over looked by Guardians and titled 'laziness' on the part of the animals - especially with horses. Further to this, these types of virus may lead to infection, again with no obvious external symptoms and then also snowball into anaemia.

This is why something as simple as fatigue should always be taken extremely seriously, as it may also indicate severe pain issues. It is hard for a Vet to make a diagnosis, when no obvious symptoms are presenting themselves. Due to the animal's Guardian being used to their normal behaviour, any slight divination from that, may well be seen and taken as a vital sign that something is wrong with them. Once presented for clinical examination it is then not uncommon for animals to be given the all clear, due to a lack of symptoms. This is where animal communication can be invaluable. It enables the animal to be able to pass on felt - but not physically presenting symptoms.

Some examples of these will be:

Feeling sick, but without physically vomiting (due to their anatomy horses can not be physically sick, but that does not prevent them from feeling sick)

Severe fatigue (an active animal may slow down only a little and feel much more tired and drained than it physically presents)

Lameness that does not become more painful upon weight baring, so the animal may not physically present as being lame.

Pain in the chest and a tickling sensation that may not present as a cough

Skin sensitivity and damaged nerve endings that may not feel worse when touched

Nerve damage or pain that in the case of a horse - may be diagnosed as a lack of correct movement due to lack of schooling.

Several years ago I went out to my stable yard to find my little Welsh pony sweating - his whole body stank. He was stood in a Laminitic stance and was shaking when only a few hours earlier, he had been presenting no symptoms at all. I called the Vet immediately, who then turned up an hour later. He injected the pony with Buscopan and then expected to leave. I stood my ground - pointed out his symptoms and told the Vet that I believed him to have an internal infection and an issue with his liver - based on his presenting symptoms. I then demanded that he be blood tested and be given antibiotics as well. The blood results came back the following morning. They showed that he had an infection and hepatitis.

My pony when I found him - was so sick, and his illness had come on so rapidly, that I had also asked to have him referred to the local hospital. I was told that my pony was not sick enough to go to hospital in a Sunday evening. How can any Vet state this when they have not even given a diagnosis? My pony was barely able to stand, he very obviously had a serious issue with his liver based upon the very strong smell coming from his body, that had manifested in a matter of a few hours. In fact, he was actually dying - he was that seriously ill. After eight long weeks on box rest (we had been having hard frost and snow so it was also not safe to let him out due to that, in light of his Laminitis) he was able to be turned back out.

He went through the summer easily, but as soon as the first frost came the following autumn, he came down with Laminitis. This was even though I stabled him for the night and went out at 11pm to give him warm water to drink. His sweat patches also had reappeared - so we had to call it a day for his sake, as he was so internally sick. This just goes to show how sick he had been that winter, and the damage caused by his illness. I have no doubt that had I not have stepped in with a diagnosis for him and demanded his correct treatment - he would have been dead by morning.

Needless to say I reported the Vet involved to the RCVS. Sadly he was let off due to his report on the visit being very different from my own truthful and correct one.

Just because someone has letters after their name or is trained and qualified in their chosen career, it does not mean integrity reins. Nor does it mean they even care about an animal. For some people no matter what their career in life, it is just that, a career. Anyone in a career within the care sector is open to falling prey to becoming mechanical and un-compassionate. Do not fall prey to allowing your heart and mind to close where the animals are concerned. The day we do, and if we do, we need to step back and choose a new career before the damage is done.

If you do not have knowledge in the physiology and the working of the bodies of animals, then my advice is to stay away from such cases. Instead, refer on to those that specialise in those areas.

We should, and must, be aiming to work with Veterinary Surgeons - not against them. We are all only human and can only do the best that we can (when and if we choose to, which sadly is not always the case). Finding and working with an open minded and willing Veterinary Surgeon, can go a long way to help animals in need and forming a good team to enable that to happen.

There are good and bad in all careers, or rather those that truly care and those that do not. It is not about the career, so much as the individual that is in that career. Needless to say, there is an alternative meaning to 'practising' in any career - rather than actually doing it.

THE SELECTIVE COMMUNICATOR

How we choose to 'hear' animals and indeed 'how' we hear them, will be through personal choice and in some cases, due to our lack of knowledge and our own biased way of thinking.

If we are closed minded and have a rigid way of thinking - meaning that when we have an opinion on something, we are not flexible to the fact what is right for one may be wrong for the next. Either through our lack of understanding that there are other ways and options, or that we do not know that those exist. We will limit our abilities within our communication skills. This will have a profoundly biased outcome to how we both hear and feel an animal express them-self.

An example of this is if we are fascinated with just one training method or therapy - think it the best thing since sliced bread and nothing can even measure up to it - we then tunnel vision ourselves. We will never allow ourselves to hear an animal state that this is the incorrect (or not the best) method to be used for them. Sadly I have seen this happen again and again, whereby Communicators advocate the same training method be used for each individual in a species. The difference in personalities and needs (need being survival and want being desire) of the individual not being taken into consideration, so the best outcome therefore is not achieved. In some cases even disaster occurring. Therapists and Trainers as well as Medical Professionals in many cases are also guilty of this.

Rather, it is of utmost importance to understand that what is truth for us, may not be for the next. Growth is about learning, exploration, education and personal experience and that within this will be found and produced the art of the unbiased and open mind. The same mind that rejects selectism on what is heard, repeated and offered to the animal's Guardian.

Sadly an open mind can not be taught; it is innate and based on experience, life path and individuality as well as personal perception. It is the art of being analytical and maintaining a quiet and well trained mind. Not conditioned - but well organised and with all information relating to others being carefully filed, to enable it to be found as and when needed.

For those truth seekers - the open minded folk, life will be a lot easier. These individuals will find themselves rarely offended by what others say. They are constantly questioning the 'why' in everything and are only to open to the fact they may be wrong. The ones that can put their hands up and say 'I could have done that better so what has it taught me, so I can do better next time round?' Understanding that each day holds lessons and knowledge with each interaction and thought. These are the explorers and seekers in life and those that will in most cases if compassion exists within them also, will likely make the best Communicators and Facilitators.

If giving an animal their true voice to the best of our ability is what we consider our role to be. Then without a doubt, we owe it not just to them, but also ourselves to get our own mind in order and our life in order to enable us to be as balanced and unbiased as possible. Not an easy task for some - but possible for those that truly seek it.

Often it is not the destination that is important on our personal journey's, but also the route that we choose to take to reach that destination and what we learn about ourselves on the way. This is the point at which positive change can be made, created and the magical mind is allowed to flourish.

AUTISM, LEARNING DIFFICULTIES AND DEMENTIA

Most species - if not all to varying degrees, will have all of the same Neuro-Peptides (emotional brain chemicals) that humans do. Not only are these emotional chemicals found in the brain, but also in the gut (Hence the term gut reaction and gut feeling, as well as stomach upset or sensation due to stress or excitement).

The mind of any individual, along with their consciousness and extremely vast and in depth nature, will have a profound effect on how they think, feel and their perception. Not forgetting the biological functioning and if you like 'wiring' of each brain that enables us all to be individuals.

Due to this as with people, animals can and do, suffer from all of the same emotional and psychological issues that we do.

Over the years it has been my privilege to work with some such individuals in animal form. From my Arabian Manta that displays Autistic like traits and learning issues, to client's animals suffering with Dementia. (Though I feel it is important to add what we may see as suffering for them may in fact be acceptable and even normal to them – they may never have experienced otherwise or even know there is an issue. The suffering in fact is sometimes only present when another is unable to meet them and understand them on their own level).

Several years ago a lady contacted me about her horse. He had a history of what at times could be considered violent behaviour. The lady in question was an experienced horse woman, but no matter what she tried, no real improvement was being seen. We chatted and she booked a consultation for her and her horse to talk to me.

To cut a long story short, from a psychological analysis of not just what the horse was 'saying' to me, his behaviour as observed by his Guardian and more importantly, what I felt that he was not saying. I was able to draw the conclusion that he was in fact somewhere on the Autistic Spectrum. I was able to discuss this with his Guardian and also throw around ideas with her on the best approach to take when interacting with him. Due to his Autism, the everyday way best suited to the average individual may not suit him, him not being average in his ability to hear and work things through in the same way another horse would.

His Guardian decided that to be 100% sure of this, she would also take the approach of having all of the relevant tests carried out, in order to exclude other causes for his behaviour. Four thousand pounds later the Vet came back with a diagnosis of Autism. His Guardian had not made the Vet aware of what I suspected until afterwards. As far as I am aware this was and still is the only actual 'diagnosis' of Autism in a horse in the UK today. There may be others and being as it is so common, I hope there is, but if there is I have yet to hear of them. However, to my way of thinking that one veterinary diagnosis speaks volumes. It shows that 'someone' in the clinical medical professional has accepted it for what it is. I hope it is just the first small step in a way forwards for further accepting animals as individuals. Especially within a world in which some in the medical profession still to this day, ignorantly deny the existence of animals having emotions. Even thought the biological and scientific evidence of their emotional chemicals and molecules are well proven.

Once again with the utmost respect I would say that if your background is not one of knowledge in psychology and mental health, or is at best 'sketchy'. In instances such as these, if you feel that you are not sure but suspect that there is a psychological issue, or one of mental health that it may fall into one of the above categories. It is best to refer the client on to someone else that is more knowledgeable in that field.

My little black Manta's issues present in several ways:

His inability to interact fully and comfortably on a consistent basis with people. This may show its self as one moment looking at you worriedly, as if he does not recognise you - to walking straight up to you with complete confidence and giving you a kiss.

A discrepancy in how and where he stores and retrieves information, by way of his long and short term memory.

The ability to understand a few training words by association, but not to associate a word with 'himself'. By this I am referring to when we call a horse by name and they acknowledge that association.

His slowed or incorrect responses to other equine's cues offered to him. These do improve in a relaxed herd environment such as the one he has living in with my other horses.

His ability to slow his heart and breath rate in times a stress and close down and remove himself both mentally and physically, to avoid mental collapse.

At times (but not consistent) consistently offering incorrect responses to cues and requests offered, even when he has learnt and correctly responded to the same requests many times before.

The Autistic Spectrum is as wide as it is long. No two personalities will consistently show and display the same characteristics. This of course can make it all the harder to fully grasp in many cases, if this is indeed the presenting cause of the problem. It is commonly believed that in the case of Autism there is a lack or absence of emotion. In fact nothing could be further from the truth. Usually the resulting behaviour is due to an inability to deal with either their own emotion's and energy, or that of others, in a way that is constructive to them. This inability may at times choose to present itself as a closing down and numbing of those emotions, to stop them being inwardly felt and outwardly expressed. This of course then results in the ability of the individual in being able lower the heart and breath rate as the emotion is not being felt. The opposite end of the scale is the animal that is unable to close themselves down in such as way, as to create emotional safe guard for themselves. Instead overflowing, mentally, energetically and thus physically into the physical explosion that we so often see, due to their inability to cope with their own emotions, those of others and what is being laid at their door in that moment in time.

Like humans, animals with Autism and learning issues need a bespoke and well considered approach in how we both physically, and emotionally communicate with them, as well as their training and interactions with others.

THE PSYCHLOGICAL SAFETY ZONE

The Psychological Safety Zone exists as much with Animal Communicators and people in general - as it does with animals. Often what is 'known' is 'safe', even if not particularly 'liked'. To give an example of this I will use my experience of helping out for a day at a primate sanctuary.

For my husband's birthday I paid for us to spend the day as 'helpers' at a Primate Sanctuary. This involved cleaning of their areas and preparing their food, as well as spending quality time with the beautiful primates that lived there. One thing that struck me immediately was the difference in their living environments. One monkey had a large grassy area and was all by himself. There was low fencing but he chose to stay within it and had plenty of freedom to roam and swing around the posts that were in there for him as his activity centre. Yet next to his playground was a small cage run type area that was fully closed in with wire, and housed quite a few smaller primates.

On first observation I wondered why one was given such freedom and was alone and yet others had such a small area and looked 'overcrowded'. It was explained to me by the Animal Psychologist that was accompanying us for the day, that the primate that was alone had previous lived his life without company. He was unable to identify with other primates and if in the company of them he would bully them. But left to his own devices and given the freedom to play and express he was neither bored nor stressed. His own little world revolved around his play area, his freedom and his ability to be able to create his own amusement and quality time in a way that suited 'him'. If introduced to others it was concerning to him to have to step out of his safety zone, in a way that he was emotionally unable to deal with.

The small cage run of primates was another story entirely. They had been rescued from a laboratory. Their life had been one of 'enclosure' with little space and with other primates close by. This had been their world and experience for so many years, that they were unable to mentally cope with 'space'. For these little guys enclosure was safe, maybe not liked, but safe. Whilst it took away their freedom to a certain extent, it was also removing the freedom they were mentally unable to cope with. This in mind their confinement was actually 'emotional kindness', that was being offered to them by those that fully understood their needs.

Next we were to visit 'Mo', another little guy that lived alone and liked to spend a lot of time in the dark shed part of his run. We were warned that Mo did not like men and that my husband was to keep his distance. I entered the enclosure area at the back of Mo's shed that was separated from the enclosure by wire. This was an area for people to greet him, well women away. He presented me with his back to scratch. Each time I stopped scratching him and turned to speak to the lady that was with us. Mo would climb across the wire wall holding on to it and quietly place his back under the palm of my hand as his cue he needed another scratch.

Then suddenly Mo went mad. He had caught a glimpse of my husband watching our interaction from around the corner. My husband quickly moved away out of sight. Mo immediately calmed and continued to move himself to ask for his scratch again. Just the visual sight of a man caused his past association of 'men equal fear and harm', had come into play. My husband was still as close so it was not Mo's olfactory system that was picking up on him in his environment. It was purely a visual observation of a man and association of what men meant to him that caused his reaction.

We can also see psychological safety zone behaviour in many other species; the ex race horse that shakes at the mere thought of leaving the confinement of his stable and is unable to deal with the vastness of the green field. To the breeding puppy farm bitch that has not seen true daylight, had grass under her feet or left the enclosure of the barn where she was likely bred herself, in many years. Not to mention those humans that have spent years cooped up in their home, barely leaving as they have been unable to deal with the outside world.

On reflection it is easy to put all of these instances into the same box. What is often failed to be seen and is so important is that, although these situations may appear to present with the same symptoms. Not all of these situations are in fact the same, regardless of following a pattern.

For some animals and people it is fear of not being able to control the fear once it is felt, that is what has caused the snowball affect. It is not necessarily the fear of the outside that is foundational to the issue. But rather, that once they are outside of their comfort zone and physically outside. Should the fear manifest, can they actually get back physically to their comfort zone? The fear of not being able to and fearing the fear may manifest, can be enough for some to want to remain to a large degree self imprisoned. What may be seen as a fear of outside and large environment, may in fact be fear by association of fear and not actually fear of anything physical other than the feeling itself.

The understanding of the true cause of such behaviour through communication is power-mount in understanding how to help the animal over come their fear. Is it even in their best interests to even over come it? As I feel it is safe to say that in some cases, what we may see as the journey to healing for that individual can in fact be psychologically breaking and a closing down of the psychological emotional state and 'self', as a coping mechanism. When this happens the fear has not really gone, it is just hidden. The healing has not really been created and what we have created in our arrogance in wanting to heal another in the wrong way, or through our naivety, is a psychologically broken closed down mind. One that appears and presents outwardly and physically as healed and in acceptance, is sadly very far from the truth.

It is for this reason that unless we have an in depth knowledge of psychology and behaviour, we have to seriously consider if these are the kind of communications that we should be engaging in at all. By not having the correct knowledge in place we could lead others to cause more harm than good, at great cost to the mind of the animal involved.

However, when our understanding of psychology and behaviour is in place and the analytical mind is at play and is able to see all sides of the coin. (Not just heads and tails, but also inside and not forgetting the outer circle that holds it all together). Then we may be in a situation where the animal and their Guardian could greatly benefit from our insight, aside from the communication. Not only this, but if we do not have the knowledge in place. Then we fall prey to hearing but not actually understanding what is being said to us by the animal. As so often it is not what they say - but what they mean. Those two important things do not always tally in a way that makes sense.

Words can be empty and can only be of use if the one hearing them understands beyond them. An animal (and indeed a person) that does not fully understand their own psychology, is not fully able to make you understand from their point of view. As the individual is unable to put how they feel into words in the depth that they need to. Therefore it is our role should we be knowledgeable enough to work with it, to 'know' the story and psychology behind those words. If we do not my advice is to steer clear and leave such communications to those that do have the knowledge needed. As the last thing we want to do is cause the animal pain, by interpreting incorrectly and advising wrongly based on our own lack of knowledge and experience. Our role is to help and aid, not hinder and cause anguish to the already fragile mind and where and how it chooses to keep itself safe and free of collapse.

SAVE THEM ALL SYNDROME

This is the term I use for those that feel the need to save 'everything' - by everything I am meaning both animals and people.

Those that scream to stop eating meat - close the slaughterhouses and stop slave labour. Not for one minute am I saying that I don't want those things to be stopped. They serve no true purpose in the grand scheme of things - or within our evolution. They are cruel, they are barbaric and those that engage in such activities are not truth seekers or the compassionate - they are the greedy. As greedy if not more so, than those that choose to buy, consume and use their products, those that enable the plight to continue. The same consumers that so often are those that are screaming for these things to come to an end and be made illegal - fancy that! Yes hypocrisy does truly rein.

Now I will draw breathe before I write the next part, please read carefully before making judgment.

If we ban factory farming tomorrow and close the slaughterhouses, what will happen to those animals already in existence?

Where will they live?

Who will feed them and pay for their food?

Who will pay for their veterinary care?

Will the farmers buy food and turn them out into lovely fields and go and stack shelves in a supermarket to pay for it all?

Will the Vets work for the rest of their lives for free, even taking on a second job to pay for the drugs they need?

Will YOU home, feed and get medical care for all of these millions of animals and people?

Provide those people with housing, food, medical care and nurture and raise the children who have lost parents in factory fires and through starvation?

If we ban factory farming right now, today, will there be enough crops already in place to feed the worlds human and animal populations, or will they face large scale starvation?

If we ban the low paid factories in China, how will those people feed themselves?

How will they find new work and income?

Who is going to fed, pay and care for all of the cats and dogs as well as other species in kill shelters. Should euthanasia due to lack of a home become illegal?

Are you going to pay for it all?

I guess not....so how can we change it other than through education over breeding and lack of spaying and neutering?

The sad truth is that humans have created a big fat mess within our world. They have caused havoc, suffering and eventually collapse should it continue.

Rather than instantly banning everything and throwing the world into even more chaos. We need to look at the foundational issues. Look to how we can create change and end the suffering long term, in such a way as we do not create more in doing so.

How can we create good pay for those working in slave labour?

How can we provide a world wide alternative to meat consumption that is both humane and long term?

How can we educate those without force to consider what is on their plate and how it got there?

How can we offer support in creating those changes?

How can we do it without judgment and the patronising of individuals?

How can we aid and not force them into wanting to create change, both for themselves and for others on a large scale?

Telling someone they are selfish is not going to cut it. Telling people they are wrong without being able to back up your reasoning is not going to swing it either. People need to work it out for themselves. They need to be supported when they feel the time for inner self exploration of themselves is needed - at the right time that it is needed and when they are ready.

As long as people fear and withdraw from waking up - change will not come. Be the person you are and can be, be the real you and lead by example. Until you are able to do this it is unfair and unjust to criticise another.

So often it is just the meeting of another individual that can cause the inspiration of some and help them see more clearly. As in the story of Claire and Bella in my book - 'From their heart to yours - Inspirational horses and the people who love them'.

It is lunch time as I sit here typing this, an average day of inspiration and smiles. Tears today also but good ones, through receiving three messages from people who feel that I have inspired them into looking to create change within themselves and what they do. Enabling them to find how they also choose to reflect that outwardly to the world as they find their true selves. That is part of my role and in some ways helping others truly find themselves and how they choose to reflect that, is my own selfish way in which fulfilment comes to me also. It creates change all round for the greater good.

There is also another element to 'Save Them All Syndrome'. That is often the role of many Animal Communicators and Healers. Often the reason that we have taken on the role as Communicators and Healers, is due to our love and compassion for animals. It is only natural to want to provide a stress free and pain free life for not only those we consider our own, but also all others, where ever they may be in the world and what ever their circumstances.

Let's take a step back from this a moment and put it into perspective.

Why are they there?

The cat not being fed correctly or not given enough food; why is he choosing to stay when it is within his ability to move on?

The horse enclosed within the paddock fencing: one that can easy jump and leave if he so chooses to. Chances are it is within his life path to be there, or he may not know anything else is out there to leave for and to. Maybe he has been institutionalised and learnt helplessness has crept in over the years. Then again....maybe quite simply it is just his choice and that for whatever reason he chooses therefore to stay.

Whatever the reason in the grand scheme of things, it is 'their' path. A reason that is valid to them and it is not for us to rush into 'every' situation and try and change it. Where that animal is may at that moment be exactly where they need to be, in order to learn and grow in their own way. If we rush in and create uninvited change in every situation that is not to our own liking, we are taking away choice from another.

We can not 'heal all', not all are meant or want to be healed. Wading in with our idealistic view of how we think another should have to live and what they should have to experience, is neither constructive to their life, or our own integrity within our work.

Nor is it constructive or kind to prolong a physical existence, when it is time to shed the outer body that is in pain and the individual's time is up. 'A short life that has been fulfilled is better than a long one empty', is my motto. Therefore when the right time has come to pass, how can we in our loving and understanding nature choose to try and override that? To inflict suffering through the forced staying of that individual that needs to go? Why instead are we not standing by their side loving them - supporting them when they need to pass in the best way we can? Instead of standing selfishly crying for ourselves and 'our' perceived 'loss'?

Instead we must choose to respect what help, or lack of help each party feels willing and able to accept, as well as the way in which they need it. It is then our role to create that offering for them, to use in such a way as they feel best for themselves. Best put, back off and let others create their own decisions as to their own welfare and how they choose to live, so long as it is not harming others. They may not yet be ready to understand in the way you do and with the perception you have, that enables you to see all possibilities. Instead stand back, support them as best you can and extend the hand of offering and friendship to them. In such a way that they know you are aiding them in their working their way towards their true self and where they need to be right now. If they need you, they will ask you - offer do not inflict.

Around four years ago I was very ill, I had lost so much weight that I was only registering at six stone.

I was weak, having dizzy spells and could barely drag myself out of bed, let alone feed myself. Yet all of this time my animals were fed and cared for, their needs met. However, as a realist I was also aware that it was only a matter of time before I would be unable to care for my horses and what that physically involved. I had recently almost passed out in a field of snow pushing a wheel barrow at 11pm one night, in a bid to get soaked hay out to my horses, so one of them would not cough. Having already bucketed the twenty buckets of water out of the bath and carried it outside as needed to soak the hay. I had to think sensibility for their sakes.

I put my property up for sale and re-homed one of my horses with a good friend. When I left him there I cried all the way home out of worry for him, even though I knew he was in safe hands. My husband pulled the car over and told me he could turn around, that we could go back and get him - I told him to keep driving. My friend bless her, told me she was not changing his passport and putting it into her name. That when the day came that I felt well enough he would still be there waiting for me. I honestly believed that day would never come and told her as much. It was the end of the road, he was hers now.

Seven weeks passed and I could barely sleep. I was worse, but I was also aware I was worse because I did not have Alfi with me. Late one night I called my friend telling her desperately that both Alfi and I needed him to come home. She replied that that was fine; she knew it would happen she just did not expect it so soon!

The following weekend we drove to collect him. From day one he had attracted a new friend whilst he was at my friend's yard. A little black Arabian named Manta. A some what confused and odd but very loveable individual - visually beautiful and inwardly even more so. Part of me felt guilty that they were having to part company - but the future as later played out was to change all of that.

Alfi arrived home and settled instantly back with his two little pony friends. Manta was never far from my mind and it was not unusual when not thinking of him for the picture of his face to come to mind, as if he was saying 'do not forget about me'.

Time passed and sadly it was time to bid a fond farewell to one of our little pony friends Meeka. She had developed a brain tumour and neurological issues had started to appear. Now there was just Alfi and his little friend Cinders. A little pony that sadly was not in the best of health - partly due to poor breeding and the greed of humans. Cinders was happy for now but she was living on borrowed time, any month could have been her last. It was time to go in search for an additional friend for Alfi and I.

I called my friend and dropped the relevant hints needed about a certain little black Arabian in her care. About a month later on a wet gusty fowl weathered day as Manta was loaded onto a trailer and arrived back at Nirvana Springs.

Manta 'called' as he stepped off the trailer, he was out of view and yet his voice was enough to cause Alfi to recognise him and prick his ears at the all familiar call. As Manta did his impressive extended trot around the summer paddock in order to assess its boundaries and all they included Alfi followed, a somewhat confused expression upon his face. Needless to say that was a few years ago now. Little Cinders has since made her way to the great beyond for the next part of her journey and Alfi and Manta still live happily side by side. Along with a new addition - Alfi's half brother, another in need named Harree, yet again a twist of destiny that I had never set out looking for. Through circumstances playing out in the right way, he was aided in finding his way home to us.

LOOKING GLASS SYNDROME

'Looking Glass Syndrome' is a term I use to explain our perception. The following is a metaphor that I use in order to explain further:

Imagine a dark land, on the land sits a house full of all of the worlds different species. The house has many different windows, each with their own unique differences. Some of the windows will be clear and have beautiful views. Some will only show darkness, some are frosted glass causing distortion and some allow you to see nothing at all. There will also be those that show the view of far away lands, mapping the horizon and allow for the playing out of scenes that we are able to observe and understand. Each one of these scenes will be different; some nice and some not so. Each window and what it has to offer is different for each individual that chooses to stand and stare.

Those in the house will find the window that suits them, the one that enables them to feel the most comfortable. Some may even choose to spend their whole life in that one position, just staring and never venturing to explore or even consider another view. In fact, they may be so static that they are not even aware that another view, another perspective is even possible and exists.

Over time some will choose to move and explore. They will go to the windows of others, enabling them to see not just in their own way, but also as others do. Some may choose to do this only once in their life time, whilst others will make it their role in life to continuously see all points of view - all windows enable them to learn and develop further.

Then we find the truth seeker; the one who has had enough of windows, views and the perceptions of both themselves and others. They believe there to be more to life and they go in search of it. Some may spend years walking around inside the house, only to come across more perceptions, more views. Only one day to find the door that leads them to the great outside. Some may be tentative, even concerned about going outside. Some may stand and wait a while until such a time as they feel ready. Others may grab the door knob and scream 'Thank goodness as I knew there was more to it!'.

When the time is right they will step outside. It may seem dark at first as only too often the distorted or perfectionist view of the windows are incorrect - as seen by those that have ventured outside. As realisation comes and the dark mists start to clear, the veil lifts and truth is now truly observed. No longer is that individual clouded, pulled down and distorted by the vision of others. They now have found the truth in what they seek and are able to see as is truly meant. They close their eyes, give acknowledgment and thanks. They then tip back their head as they open their eyes and they see the sky. 'WOW....this is only the very beginning of the awakening'.

The truth is that not all individuals have the strength of mind to venture outside and some may just be happy within their own perception and their 'lot'. It does not make them bad individuals, nor does it make them stupid. It is just where they are on their life path and within their fragile psyche. It will be dependant on life lessons that they have chosen to reject or to take on board willingly and what their early experiences have both offered and denied them.

The meat eater that declares he loves eating meat will likely never make it out of the house. He will likely never reach the window that offers the slaughterhouse scene. Those that are unable to cope with the death of a loved one will likely never see the sight of the funeral directors back room - they will choose not to venture to that window.

However, when we choose to explore all elevations and all windows, we are able to acknowledge each for what they are. We can do so without having to close our eyes to misery and the plight of others due to an inability to cope with our own emotions. Instead, we will be able to understand how they feel, why they think the way they do and we will be able to find some kind of peace within it. Knowing that is them, we do not need to be like them if we do not choose to be. We can find another perspective and choose to look through the clear windows and then look to the skies for the answers.

No two individuals will be the same; how can they be? Each of their life paths will have offered different life lessons, different circumstances and events. Each of these will have offered them a way to move forwards and even the option to hold back.

The psyche can be fragile; some are already broken beyond repair as shown by our psychiatric words and the sadly disturbed individuals they home, and those that choose to hide in their houses, stable or kennel as the outside world is just too over whelming. Often these are the ones that chose to venture outside too quickly, enabling them to explore too many windows and perceptions first, as well as those forced out with little understanding of others and how and why they do the things that they do to each other - the agoraphobic racing horse; to the abused child and the dog used as bait for fighting dogs.

However, there will be those that know that whatever life has thrown at them - does not have to shape them. They understand that they are not their circumstances or their experiences, but that innately there is more. These are the survivors in life, the ones that choose to heal and can heal to varying degrees by facing their fears, their challenges ahead and wanting to overcome the uncomfortable feeling that exists in the moment. They do this In the full knowledge that life in its entirety is waiting for them. Those individuals are those that I hold the most respect for, those that have found the inner strength to throw caution to the wind - those that feel the fear and do it anyway. These are the warriors of life that will help to bring through a whole new generation of believers in 'self'.

This does not mean for one moment I hold any form of disrespect whatsoever for those that have not ventured outside. Rather, I see where they are in their life and in their own minds, as where they need to be and within their coping with life. But as a truth seeker and having known the journey to get here, I know the struggles and what it entails. Any that choose to tread that path have my greatest respect and support.

SYMPATHY VS EMPATHY

What we choose to work and how we think will have a huge impact on our emotional state when we are working with horses. Also, how we view them and how we cope with their illnesses and 'passings', as well as our emotional issues surrounding them.

Simply put, when we choose to work with sympathy, we leave ourselves open to be dragged into another's drama. We allow our own emotions to be affected by those of others. We finish our work, leave the company of that horse or person and we feel awful. We feel sad for their pain and we are worried about them. We can even have trouble sleeping through having them 'on our mind'. Whilst there is nothing wrong with sympathy in as much as it shows only too well the level of compassion innate to us, it does not serve us and nor is it positive for our own emotional health. It does not help the horses and people that may need our help and support and need us to be fully focused and present when we are in their company. If we are left worrying about a horse, that will be on our mind and our focus is not fully directed in the area that it needs to be when we are in the company of others. There are even instances when some horses and people may even feel patronised by another's sympathy towards them.

However, when we choose to work with empathy, this enables us to understand how the horse feels. At the same time it enables us to be able to safely guide our own emotions in such a way that we do not take the horse's negativity, or sorrow upon ourselves. This enables us to support the individual with a positive outlook and approach, enabling us to help and inspire, as well as seeing the positive within a negative experience. It will stop us from being drained by their personal drama. By drama I am not insinuating in a patronising manner that they are creating drama. But rather, through circumstance, drama has manifested, not necessarily instigated by them and which may be beyond their control.

Empathy is supporting and creating an ideal that lacks and holds no agenda in changing another's life path, or interfering with it. It is the art of being able to play the observer, to watch, hear and understand what is playing out - without becoming directly involved. Working with empathy as the observer also enables us to stand back and see the bigger picture, rather than being directly emotionally involved. It aids us in being able to see things are they truly are and objectively. It enables us to view through the distortion of emotions, removing biased approach and outcome and gets us right to the heart of the matter.

When we let go of ego and we are able to step back without the need to be overly involved emotionally, we are able to deal with much needed matters at hand in a calm and constructive way. This may be emergency restraining of a horse for their own safety in the case of serious injury, to the ability to stand with a horse as he passes, without crying or bombarding him with any form of negative emotion on our part, due to how we may otherwise be feeling.

In instances such as these we are then able to keep our head, keep our breath and heart rate low and safely manage our own energy. This will benefit the horse in question no end, because it is coming from a place of empathy rather than a state of just not caring. It will carry the correct vibration, feel authentic and be of no end of benefit to the horse, enabling them the opportunity to synchronise with our own brain wave state and other physiological functions that will further aid them in maintaining their own calmness in how they deal with their presenting situation.

Imagine a bubble around each individual; each bubble being the energy of their emotions. When we choose to allow that bubble to come into contact with our own and we invade another's emotional energy, it mixes with our own – this is sympathy. We then enable it to distort our own emotional state. The art of empathy however, is when we choose to stand back and observe and read the energy of emotions. We can then see them with clarity. Our own emotional state is intact and we are not distorting the energy of emotions for another individual with our own should a negative mindset prevail within us at any given time.

So for the sake of yourself and the horse whose company you are in please choose to work with empathy over sympathy. They will thank you for it.

I feel it is also important to point out sentience within empathy and how this can cause us to still feel the horse's emotions when we are in the company of a horse, in the same way that they are affected by us through our breath rate, brain wave state and other biological functions. We too will be affected by theirs and this can in many cases cause a change in our own mental and emotional state. This is very different from sympathy and does not automatically mean that it is sympathy that we are experiencing. Rather, this is just a normal physical reaction to the environment that we have found ourselves in. If we are working with empathy then when we remove ourselves from the company of the horse, our body will physically change back to how it was before, as it is no longer synchronising with the biological functions of the horse that is feeling emotionally uncomfortable.

ABOUT THE AUTHOR

Holly has been working as a professional Animal Communicator since 1999. She currently lives in Wales with her seven cats and three Arabian horses.

She is the Author of many books and courses on animal therapies. These are available throughout the UK as well as internationally.

She has a keen interest in natural behaviour and medicine, as well as psychological disorders in animals and Neuroscience. A huge amount of her time is spent helping people to understand their animals - aid in their recovery and create a better life for them.

Holly was one of the first Animal Communicators to teach workshops in UK and is the Author of the first recognised Animal Communication Diploma in the UK.

Her accredited courses are available through Stonebridge College, links for which can be found on her website.

<u>www.hollydavis.co.uk</u>

Holly's Animal Healing Workshop CD is also available through her website. This CD is highly recommended for those who wish to learn Animal Communication. As it contains guided instructions to follow to enable you to make a connection with animals.

FREDA

Freda was 18 months old and had not long had her second litter of kittens when we re-homed her from a rescue along with her daughter Willow, that was from her first litter.

Three months later she was shot. An inch and a half of bone has shattered in one of her hind legs which had to be amputated. Her foot was broken on her other hind.

Freda was not angry with the person that did this to her. Rather she was sad that this person had so little love and compassion in their heart and therefore their life.

"If we wish to help animals to heal. We must first heal our own ignorance and lack of knowledge that is keeping them sick."

Printed in Great Britain
by Amazon.co.uk, Ltd.,
Marston Gate.